BODY WISDOM THROUGH
RED LIGHT THERAPY

A Brighter Path to Wellness to Fight Inflammation and Aging, Amplify Energy, Aid in Weight Loss, and Support Skin Rejuvenation and Cellular Renewal

Grace Bailey

Published by Bailey Premier Publishing LLC
Canadian, Texas 79014

ISBN 978-1-996543-10-7 Paperback
ISBN 978-1-966543-11-4 (Kindle/Epub)
ISBN 978-1-966543-12-1 Hardback
ISBN 978-1-966543-13-8 Audio

Disclaimer:
The author is not a licensed or certified practitioner of Somatic Therapy. The exercises and practices shared in this book are based on personal experience and the positive results achieved through their use. This book is intended for educational and informational purposes only and should not be considered professional medical or therapeutic advice. Please consult a licensed healthcare professional before beginning any new therapeutic or exercise regimen, especially if you have any medical conditions or concerns.

Legal Notice:
The author and publisher of this book disclaim any liability for any injury, loss, or damage resulting from the use or misuse of the information contained within. The content provided is not a substitute for professional care, and all readers are encouraged to seek advice from a qualified healthcare provider. By using the exercises and information in this book, you acknowledge that you are participating at your own risk and accept full responsibility for any outcomes.

CONTENTS

FREE Companion Journal Included!

Supercharge Your Red Light Therapy Results

As a thank-you for reading *Body Wisdom through Red Light Therapy*, I've created a beautiful, printable **Companion Journal + Weekly Tracker**—designed to help you stay consistent, reflect on your progress, and make the most of every session.

Inside you'll find:

- Daily logs to track sessions, duration, and goals

- Weekly reflections for mood, pain, and energy

- Notes section for sound therapy, meditation, or personal insights

- A quick-start guide for choosing the right wavelengths

Get Instant Access Now:

subscribepage.io/Free_RedLightTherapy_Companion_Journal

Just enter your email, then click the *Free Copy* link to be redirected to the free download.

Your healing journey is personal. Let this tracker be your guide.

With gratitude,
Grace Bailey

INTRODUCTION

WELCOME TO THE THIRD and next installment in the *Body Wisdom* series. If you've journeyed through *Body Wisdom Through Somatic Therapy* and *Body Wisdom Through Sound Therapy*, this volume provides another path to deeper healing. Though each book stands on its own, together they offer a holistic and integrated approach to personal well-being.

In the pursuit of optimal health, few tools offer the versatility of red light therapy. It has the potential to rejuvenate skin, boost energy, support weight management, and reduce inflammation—all through a noninvasive, science-backed approach. Rooted in modern innovation and time-honored healing traditions, this therapy is reshaping how we approach wellness.

I first encountered red light therapy during one of my regular massage sessions a few years ago. I had been treating myself to massages to help manage persistent back pain. During one visit, my massage therapist, Vanessa, incorporated a red light into the treatment. I didn't notice a change right away, but after a few sessions, I was amazed to find that a small, hard lump that had developed on my chest over several months had vanished entirely.

That experience set me on a path to learn more. I delved into the science behind red light therapy, eager to understand how it worked. This book is the culmination of that journey. It serves as a guide to help you discover the benefits that I, and many others, have experienced.

The purpose of this book is straightforward. My goal is to provide you with an easy-to-understand guide to using red light therapy. This book is backed by scientific evidence and offers insights that can help you improve your health and well-being. Whether you're new to this therapy or have some experience, you'll find valuable information in these pages.

Red light therapy stands at the forefront of modern health solutions. Its versatility is remarkable. It addresses inflammation, one of the root causes of many chronic health issues. It aids in combating the visible signs of aging, rejuvenating skin, and promoting cellular health. It can enhance energy levels, support weight management, and offer a natural approach to improving overall wellness.

The science supporting red light therapy is robust. Studies have shown its effectiveness across various health domains. For instance, research indicates its potential to enhance mitochondrial function, the powerhouse of our cells. This breakthrough underscores why this therapy is gaining attention from scientists and health enthusiasts alike.

As you turn the pages of this book, you will embark on a journey. Each chapter builds on the previous one, guiding you from foundational knowledge to practical application. You'll learn the science behind red light therapy, strategies to integrate it into your daily routine, and the best ways to measure its impact on your health.

Who is this book for? It's for anyone seeking alternative health solutions. It's for those interested in anti-aging, wellness, and holistic health practices. Whether you're a health professional or looking to enhance your wellness, you'll find this book insightful and valuable.

I encourage you to embrace red light therapy to enhance your wellness journey. Explore the possibilities it offers. Commit to incorporating the insights from this book into your life. The potential benefits are vast, and the journey is yours to take.

As we continue, consider this: What if the key to a healthier, more vibrant life was as simple as light? This book will explore that possibility, offering stories and evidence that shed light on how red light therapy can transform your health. Let's walk this path together and discover what awaits.

Chapter 1

UNDERSTANDING RED
LIGHT THERAPY

Red light therapy helps activate the body's own healing mechanisms by improving cellular energy.

–DR. MICHAEL HAMBLIN

THAT CALMING FEELING YOU get while watching a sunset isn't just in your imagination—light has a measurable effect on the human body. Red light therapy builds on this idea by using specific wavelengths to stimulate healing and enhance well-being. But what exactly makes this red light so effective? And how does it interact with our biology?

The Science of Light: How Red Light Therapy Works

The electromagnetic spectrum spans a wide range of wavelengths and includes all the colors of visible light. Red light is special in this spectrum, falling between roughly 620 and 750 nanometers. This range allows it to penetrate biological tissues more deeply than most visible light wavelengths. This penetration is the key to its therapeutic potential because it allows red light to reach deeper layers of skin and muscle, facilitating healing and rejuvenation at a cellular level.

Photobiomodulation (PBM) may not be a widely known term, but it describes an impressive biological response: When cells absorb specific wavelengths of light, they activate processes that support healing and vitality. In particular, red light stimulates the mitochondria—often compared to engines within the cell—boosting their efficiency and promoting better cellular function.

Red light stimulates the production of adenosine triphosphate (ATP), the fuel that powers every cell in the body. When ATP levels rise, cells become better at healing, performing, and growing. And that's just part of the picture. Red light also helps keep reactive oxygen species in check, lowering oxidative stress and promoting healthier cells.

So, what does that all mean in practical terms? Reactive oxygen species (ROS) are highly reactive molecules that contain oxygen, and they're a normal byproduct of cellular energy production in the mitochondria. At low levels, ROS contribute to essential functions like immune defense, cell signaling, and wound healing. However, when ROS accumulate in excess, they can cause oxidative stress, harming cells and genetic material. Red light therapy plays a key role in modulating ROS; it supports balance without eliminating these important molecules altogether.

Red light therapy's history is rooted in groundbreaking science. In the 1990s, NASA studied how light affected plant growth in space and inadvertently discovered its healing benefits for human tissue. Red and near-infrared light accelerated wound healing and boosted cell growth in lab settings. These early findings laid the foundation for medical research into its broader therapeutic uses.

Central to this technology is the enzyme cytochrome c oxidase, a vital component of the cellular respiration process. When red light is absorbed by the cells, it activates this enzyme, enhancing its efficiency and increasing energy production. This interaction strengthens the cell's ability to function and repair. Cytochrome c oxidase is the conduit that translates light energy into biological activity, essentially turning photons into fuel for the body.

What began in NASA's labs has become a trusted tool in modern wellness. Though red light therapy was once met with doubt, continued research has proven its value and dispelled early misconceptions. Its impact reaches far beneath the skin, supporting mitochondrial health, optimizing the body's natural energy systems, and bringing lasting benefits for energy, recovery, and overall well-being.

As you read this book, you'll see how the science behind red light therapy connects to real-life benefits. Each chapter builds on this foundation, offering practical tips and research-backed insights. Whether your goal is to reduce inflammation, increase energy, or improve skin health, red light therapy can help you get there.

Consider the possibilities: How could harnessing the power of light change your approach to wellness? The answer lies within the pages ahead, where science meets simplicity and potential becomes reality. Understanding how red light therapy works will give you knowledge and the tools to take charge of your well-being.

Cellular Renewal: The Power of Photobiomodulation

Supple skin, faster recovery, and renewed vitality are more than just aesthetic benefits—they're signs of deep cellular support. Red light therapy, through photobiomodulation, taps into your body's natural healing abilities by working beneath the surface to restore balance and spark regeneration.

A standout benefit of red light therapy is its ability to boost collagen production. Collagen is the framework that supports firm, youthful skin. When red light reaches the skin, it activates fibroblasts—the cells that produce collagen—prompting them to ramp up activity. The result is smoother, more radiant skin with fewer fine lines and scars.

Beyond collagen production, red light therapy addresses inflammation—an underlying factor in many chronic conditions. While inflammation is a natural part of healing, persistent inflammation can lead to tissue damage. Red light therapy helps regulate cytokine activity, reducing excessive inflammatory responses. This cytokine regulation promotes healthier skin and greater cellular resilience, enhancing the body's ability to withstand oxidative stress and external challenges.

To fully appreciate these benefits, it is helpful to explore the specific cellular pathways influenced by red light therapy. One critical pathway is NF-kB, a protein complex that regulates immune response and inflammation. By modulating this pathway, red light therapy helps maintain balance within the cell, preventing overactive inflammatory responses that can damage tissues. Additionally, it alters the JAK/STAT signaling pathway, which helps cells "hear" messages from cytokines and turn those messages into action. This is integral in processes like cell growth and immune function. By fine-tuning these pathways, red light therapy supports overall cellular health and functionality.

Consistent use of this therapy brings long-term benefits that echo throughout the body's systems. Regular exposure to red light improves cellular turnover—a process akin to giving your cells a fresh start. As new ones swiftly replace old cells, tissues remain healthy and robust. This cellular renewal can even delay signs of aging at a cellular level. It's not meant to turn back the clock but help you maintain optimal cell function as time progresses.

Consider the impact on someone juggling a busy lifestyle, perhaps a teacher standing in front of students all day or a nurse working long shifts. Consistent red light therapy sessions could mean fewer aches from standing all day and quicker recovery from minor injuries—a tangible improvement in quality of life. This constant renewal and repair ensure that cells remain in peak condition, ready to face whatever challenges come.

Chronic inflammation is linked to diseases like arthritis and diabetes, so managing it becomes crucial for long-term health. Red light therapy's role here is preventative as much as it is restorative, strengthening cellular defenses against potential threats.

Incorporating this therapy into your routine is quite simple. It involves setting aside time each morning or evening for a brief session, like brushing your teeth or taking vitamins. The key lies in consistency—making it a part of your daily ritual to reap cumulative benefits over time.

The beauty of red light therapy is in its subtlety; it works quietly yet effectively, supporting your body's natural processes without invasive procedures or harsh chemicals. It's akin to having an invisible helper that boosts your biological resilience from within.

This quiet efficiency is complemented by insights from diverse research fields, gradually unfolding its full potential as an integrative component of holistic health. A certain empowerment comes from leveraging such technology—knowing that you're actively supporting your body's health in a safe, noninvasive way. As you delve deeper into this book, you'll discover more about how red light therapy can seamlessly integrate into your life, offering a path to health that is both modern and rooted in science.

Anti-Aging and Skin Health: Reducing Wrinkles Naturally

Red light therapy goes beyond surface beauty, helping restore the skin's underlying vitality. It naturally reduces wrinkles and enhances skin tone by increasing collagen and elastin production. Collagen serves as the skin's structural framework, promoting firmness and elasticity. When red light penetrates the skin, it activates fibroblasts—cells responsible for collagen synthesis—leading to a smoother, more even complexion. Elastin, another essential protein, helps skin retain its shape and resilience. Together, these effects promote a youthful, revitalized appearance from the inside out.

Scientific evidence supports these anti-aging claims. Dermatological studies have shown significant improvements in skin texture and elasticity following consistent use of red light therapy.

One clinical trial observed participants using red light devices three times a week for 12 weeks. The results were impressive: Participants reported smoother skin and a reduction in wrinkle depth. Peer-reviewed trials back these findings, demonstrating measurable changes in skin health and appearance.

Beyond wrinkles, red light therapy addresses a variety of skin conditions. It effectively reduces acne by minimizing inflammation and bacteria on the skin's surface. This reduction leads to fewer breakouts and clearer skin over time. Red light therapy also offers relief for those with rosacea, a condition characterized by redness and visible blood vessels. Calming inflammation diminishes redness, creating a more even skin tone. These benefits make it a versatile tool for managing common dermatological issues.

Incorporating red light therapy into your skincare routine can be straightforward. Consider it a complement to your existing regimen rather than a replacement. For morning routines, start with a brief session of red light therapy before applying sunscreen and makeup. This approach allows the light to penetrate clean skin without interference from topical products. Integrate it after cleansing but before applying serums or moisturizers in the evening. This timing ensures that the skin absorbs active ingredients more effectively post-therapy.

Another advantage of red light therapy is its compatibility with topical treatments. It enhances the absorption of skincare products, making them more effective. For instance, using a vitamin C serum after a session can amplify its brightening effects. Similarly, combining red light therapy with anti-aging creams that contain retinol or peptides maximizes their benefits, promoting smoother and firmer skin.

Years of dealing with stubborn acne can be frustrating, especially when conventional treatments fail to deliver lasting results. For one individual, incorporating red light therapy marked a turning point. Inflammation and bacteria decreased, and within weeks, their skin looked visibly clearer—without the need for harsh chemicals. This kind of transformation shows the potential of merging science and skincare in a gentle and effective way.

Skin Health Checklist

Below is an easy-to-follow skincare regimen that incorporates red light therapy:

Step	Product/Tool	When to Use	Purpose	Notes
Cleanse	Gentle facial cleanser	Morning & Evening	Removes dirt, oil, and makeup	Choose based on skin type (hydrating, balancing, etc.)
Tone	Alcohol-free toner	Morning & Evening	Balances pH, preps skin for next steps	Optional if skin is sensitive
Treat (AM)	Vitamin C serum	Morning	Brightens skin, protects against free radicals	Follow with SPF
Moisturize (AM)	Lightweight moisturizer	Morning	Hydrates and protects skin	Look for hyaluronic acid or ceramides
Red Light Therapy	Red light therapy device (LED panel, mask, or wand)	Morning or Evening	Reduces inflammation, boosts collagen, improves tone	Use on clean, dry skin for 5–20 min, 3–5x/week
Sunscreen	Broad-spectrum SPF 30+	Morning	Shields skin from UV damage	Use daily, even on cloudy days
Treat (PM)	Retinol or targeted serum	Evening	Supports cell turnover, addresses acne or aging	Start with 2–3x/week, then increase as tolerated
Moisturize (PM)	Rich night cream or facial oil	Evening	Locks in moisture and nourishes skin overnight	Choose based on skin needs (anti-aging, soothing, etc.)
Exfoliate	Gentle exfoliant (enzyme or acid-based)	1–2x/week (PM)	Removes dead skin cells, improves absorption	Avoid on red light therapy days if skin is sensitive
Mask	Hydrating or clarifying mask	1x/week (PM)	Deep treatment tailored to skin concerns	Follow with moisturizer

The benefits of red light therapy go beyond improving appearance. Consistent use supports overall skin health by enhancing cellular turnover and building resistance to environmental stress. This strengthened resilience is reflected in a more radiant look and skin that feels softer, more hydrated, and less reactive. Incorporating red light therapy into a regular routine encourages a proactive, empowered approach to long-term skin wellness.

Invasive treatments are often seen as the default solution for aging skin, but red light therapy offers a gentler, science-backed alternative. It allows you to naturally support your skin's health without extreme interventions. Embracing this technology means investing in your well-being conveniently and confidently from home.

As you continue exploring this book, you'll uncover more ways to leverage red light therapy's capabilities across different aspects of health and wellness. Whether you want to enhance your skincare routine or address specific concerns, this therapy offers a personalized approach that aligns with your needs.

Energy Amplification: Boosting Vitality with Light

Every cell in your body runs on adenosine triphosphate (ATP), which you can think of as the fuel in your car's engine. Without it, nothing moves, and nothing functions. When your cells produce ATP efficiently, you feel energized and ready to take on the world. Red light therapy plays a crucial role in this process. By stimulating the production of ATP, it amplifies your body's natural energy. It's like turning up the wattage on a light bulb, making everything shine brighter and work better. This increase in cellular energy translates into enhanced stamina and endurance, whether you're running a marathon or just getting through a busy day at work.

Red light therapy can significantly affect energy levels. With regular use, it may help ease chronic fatigue and support sustained vitality throughout the day. Instead of relying on stimulants like caffeine, many individuals experience a natural boost in energy that improves focus and stamina. This renewed sense of vitality comes from improved cellular energy metabolism, where cells become more efficient at turning nutrients into usable fuel, helping to reduce fatigue and enhance daily performance.

Countless individuals have shared powerful testimonials about the benefits of red light therapy. Athletes, for instance, often report faster recovery and enhanced endurance. A competitive cyclist determined to improve race performance might find that incorporating light therapy into their regimen helps reduce muscle fatigue and improve training outcomes. But it's not limited to athletes. Busy parents, balancing work and family life, often experience increased energy and focus, allowing them to move through their day with greater ease and vitality.

Optimizing red light therapy sessions for energy benefits involves understanding the ideal frequency and duration. Start with short sessions to maximize results, gradually increasing as your body adapts. For instance, beginning with 10-minute sessions three times a week can be effective. Consistency is key here; regular exposure ensures that cells continue producing ATP efficiently. Timing also plays a role—morning sessions can set a positive tone for the day ahead. In contrast, evening sessions may help you unwind after a long day without disrupting your sleep patterns.

Incorporating red light therapy into your routine doesn't require drastic changes. It could mean setting aside time during your lunch break or unwinding with a session after dinner. This therapy's adaptability allows it to fit seamlessly into various lifestyles, whether you're an early riser or a night owl. With each session, you're investing in your body's energy reserves, creating a surplus that powers you through life's demands.

For those seeking to enhance their daily productivity, red light therapy offers a natural solution. It's akin to having an internal battery charger that keeps you running smoothly without the crashes associated with caffeine or sugar highs. This sustainable energy boost fosters a sense of well-being and efficiency, helping you achieve more with less effort.

Take, for instance, the story of an office worker who used to hit a wall every afternoon. After adding red light therapy to their routine, they began to feel more focused and energized throughout the day. The usual cravings for sugary snacks disappeared, and that familiar brain fog lifted, replaced by a steady flow of energy that made their workday more manageable.

As you explore the possibilities of red light therapy for energy amplification, consider the potential it holds for your personal wellness journey. It doesn't just help you feel more energetic—it allows you to live life to its fullest, with the vitality to pursue passions and dreams without exhaustion holding you back.

By adopting these practices, you're boosting energy levels and contributing to improved overall health. The benefits extend beyond just feeling awake; they encompass enhanced mood, better cognitive function, and even greater physical performance. With red light therapy as part of your wellness arsenal, you can tap into an inexhaustible source of energy that empowers you to live vibrantly and accomplish more than you ever thought possible.

Red light therapy's potential for increasing stamina and reducing fatigue is vast, inviting you to explore its transformative effects on your vitality with curiosity and openness.

Weight Loss and Metabolism: Shedding Pounds With Red Light

Weight loss often feels complex, but red light therapy introduces a supportive, science-based approach. By stimulating the breakdown of fat and enhancing how your body uses energy, it helps activate your natural fat-burning pathways. This metabolic boost can lead to improved calorie burning—even while you're at rest—offering a gentle yet powerful way to support your wellness and fitness goals.

The combination of red light therapy and exercise offers a highly effective approach to supporting weight loss and performance. When used alongside physical activity, red light therapy enhances fat oxidation, allowing the body to use stored fat more efficiently as fuel. This supports weight reduction and boosts endurance during workouts. After exercise, it helps speed up recovery by easing muscle soreness and reducing inflammation, enabling more consistent and effective training sessions.

Scientific research supports these claims with tangible evidence. Controlled weight loss trials have shown promising results, with participants experiencing more significant reductions in body fat compared to those who did not use red light therapy. In one study, individuals who combined the therapy with regular exercise lost more inches around their waist and hips than those who exercised alone.

Personal success stories abound as well. Consider someone who struggled with stubborn belly fat despite maintaining a healthy diet and workout routine. After incorporating red light therapy into their regimen, they noticed a significant reduction in waist size and an overall improvement in body composition.

When using red light therapy for weight loss, it's essential to separate fact from fiction. The therapy encourages fat loss, but this doesn't always mean immediate weight loss on the scale. Factors like water retention and increased muscle mass can influence your weight. To track progress, focus instead on body measurements or the way your clothes fit. Most importantly, aim for sustainable changes and a healthier lifestyle over time—there are no overnight solutions.

Red light therapy isn't a magic fix, but it *is* a powerful ally. To get the best results, think of it as part of your broader wellness plan, not a standalone solution.

Here's how to make it work for you:

Pair it with movement:

Use red light therapy before or after your workout. A quick session beforehand can help wake up your metabolism and prepare your body for energy use. Post-workout, it can reduce inflammation and support faster recovery.

Stay consistent:

Aim for 3–5 sessions per week. Just like exercise or healthy eating, results come from showing up regularly—not going all in for a week and then stopping.

Fuel your body well:

Combine red light therapy with balanced nutrition. Your cells need quality nutrients to produce energy and heal—light helps them do this better, but food is the fuel.

Track what matters:

Don't obsess over the scale. Instead, track how you feel, how your clothes fit, or how quickly your body recovers. Progress is more than a number.

Misconceptions often stem from overhyped promises and unrealistic expectations set by those selling miracle solutions. It's vital to approach red light therapy with a balanced perspective—one that acknowledges its potential while understanding its limitations. This therapy does not replace healthy habits but rather enhances them, making your efforts more effective and rewarding.

Red light therapy brings a modern, science-backed approach to weight management that aligns with today's holistic wellness philosophies. It offers a safe, natural way to support your body's internal processes and become more actively engaged in your health journey.

As you continue reading, consider how this therapy could enhance your lifestyle. Could it be the supportive tool you've been seeking? Everyone's path to wellness is unique. Red light therapy can serve as a gentle guide toward improved energy, balance, and long-term vitality.

Chapter 2

ADDRESSING COMMON CONCERNS AND MISCONCEPTIONS

Photobiomodulation is not just light exposure; it's targeted cellular rejuvenation.

–DR. HARRY WHELAN

Debunking Myths: Separating Fact From Fiction

THERAPIES CLAIMING TO BE universal cures often attract curiosity and skepticism—and rightly so. While red light therapy offers a range of benefits supported by scientific research, it has also been surrounded by myths and misinformation. To better understand its true potential, let's examine some of the most common misconceptions and explore what's backed by solid evidence.

Many people mistakenly associate red light therapy with UV tanning because both involve lying under lights. But the science behind them couldn't be more different. UV light is known to damage skin and raise cancer risks. On the other hand, red light is completely non-ionizing, which means it doesn't have enough energy to harm your DNA or skin. Instead, it works by gently penetrating the skin, helping the body heal and renew itself. Knowing the difference helps clarify why red light therapy is safe and widely used for wellness.

A common misconception is that red light therapy is a miracle solution that instantly cures all ailments. This belief often stems from exaggerated marketing that overstates its effects. While the therapy does offer notable benefits—such as improved skin health and enhanced energy—it's not a cure-all. Its true power lies in being part of a broader wellness strategy. Red light therapy works best when integrated into a consistent health routine rather than used as a standalone solution.

In our information-saturated world, truth and exaggeration often coexist online. Forums and social media can be powerful tools but also allow myths and misinformation to spread quickly. Marketing tactics may further distort reality by presenting inflated claims to drive consumer interest. It's essential to question bold promises and seek out evidence-based resources to make informed decisions. Trust grows from clarity, and verifying claims through research or trusted experts ensures you're guided by facts, not fiction.

Beyond the misconceptions of what red light therapy is, misunderstandings exist regarding who can use it. The myth that red light therapy is only for athletes or those with specific ailments disregards its potential broad spectrum of uses. Whether someone wants to refresh their skin or manage the emotional effects of seasonal changes, red light therapy offers meaningful benefits. Its ability to support physical and emotional well-being makes it a valuable and adaptable tool for many.

Checklist to Use for Researching Credible Sources

Navigating the wealth of information online can be daunting. Below is a checklist that provides questions to ask and information to look for as you review the information available for red light therapy research:

Checklist for Identifying Credible Health Resources

- Look for **peer-reviewed scientific journals** with research evaluated by experts in the field. You will find many such reports in the Reference section at the end of the book.

- **Consult healthcare professionals** for guidance that aligns with your personal health goals.

- When reading online content, check if the source **cites scientific studies or expert analyses**.

- Verify that articles include **references or links to original research** for transparency.

- Prioritize websites with domains like **".edu"**, **".gov"**, or **".org"**, which are generally more reliable.

- Be cautious with commercial sites using **".com" or ".co"** if they lack citations or scientific backing.

- Stay alert to **overly sensational claims** that promise quick fixes without evidence.

- Use these strategies to separate **factual information from myths**, supporting informed decisions about your health.

By clearing up misconceptions, we can better appreciate red light therapy for what it truly offers—a gentle, supportive addition to a healthy lifestyle. Understanding its potential and boundaries helps us use it wisely and purposefully as part of our overall wellness plan.

Understanding red light therapy begins with knowledge—and knowledge is power. The more you learn about its benefits and boundaries, the more confidently and safely you can use it. By the end of this chapter, you will have the clarity you need to confidently move forward, cutting through confusion and deepening your understanding.

Overcoming Skepticism: Scientific Evidence and Case Studies

A healthy dose of skepticism often accompanies any new health innovation, and that's good. Asking questions and seeking evidence is part of making informed choices. As interest in red light therapy expands, it has also come under the microscope, sparking curiosity and debate.

Despite initial skepticism, a growing body of scientific research strongly supports the effectiveness of red light therapy. Numerous studies have documented its significant therapeutic benefits. Clinical trials, for example, have shown notable success in reducing pain levels, particularly for individuals with chronic conditions. One such study reported substantial pain relief following consistent treatment sessions, pointing to the therapy's promising role as a noninvasive approach to pain management.

The effectiveness of red light therapy has been documented across a variety of demographic groups and health challenges. For athletes, it has emerged as a potent tool to enhance recovery, enabling a quicker return to training post-competition. Indeed, studies have highlighted reductions in fatigue and improvement in muscle performance, underscoring its value in sports medicine.

In addition to its pain-relieving effects, red light therapy has shown significant benefits for skin health. Studies report improvements in skin texture and elasticity, offering a gentle, noninvasive alternative to traditional cosmetic procedures. These results provide an appealing option for individuals seeking to naturally enhance their skin, without using needles or harsh treatments. This underscores the therapy's versatility and growing appeal among those who prefer a more holistic approach to skincare.

Emerging evidence suggests that red light therapy could extend its impact into mental and emotional wellness. By stimulating brain activity linked to relaxation and improved mood, it may offer support for those dealing with stress or anxiety. Although further research is needed, these early insights present a promising step toward more holistic approaches to mental health care. Below is a summary of how red light therapy may be impacting mood:

How Red Light Therapy Might Support Mood:

- **Boosts mitochondrial function:**

RLT enhances energy production in brain cells, which may improve mental clarity, alertness, and emotional stability.

- **Reduces inflammation:**

Chronic inflammation is linked to mood disorders. RLT's anti-inflammatory effects may support emotional regulation and stress response.

- **Improves sleep quality:**

RLT can help regulate circadian rhythms and melatonin production, promoting better sleep, which is a key factor in emotional well-being.

- **Promotes relaxation:**

Many users report a calming effect after sessions, possibly due to reduced muscle tension and nervous system support.

Personal experiences often mirror what the science shows, offering powerful reminders of red light therapy's real-world impact. Take Rachel, for example, a woman living with chronic back pain who found little relief through conventional treatments. After a few weeks of consistent red light therapy, her pain eased significantly, allowing her to return to activities she had long avoided. Her journey is one of many. Athletes, too, turn to this therapy to enhance performance and speed up recovery—whether it's a marathon runner shaving minutes off their time or a weightlifter pushing past former limits without lingering soreness.

Research continues to play a pivotal role in affirming red light therapy's effects over time. Ongoing longitudinal studies explore sustaining benefits and emerging areas of application. Collaborations with medical research centers ensure that findings are both credible and adaptable to real-world scenarios. This union of science with clinical application fortifies the therapy's credibility, swaying skeptics and encouraging broader acceptance among enthusiasts.

Balancing skepticism with openness is vital in exploring red light therapy. Being critical does not imply outright dismissal of new concepts; rather, it entails assessing emerging evidence with an educated lens. New studies may reshape our perception of this therapy's full potential, so staying well-informed is key. Personal experiences, too, contribute to a deeper understanding. While science provides the framework, individual stories add nuance and richness to our grasp of its impacts.

Integrating scientific research and personal experience is vital when evaluating any health practice. A well-rounded understanding comes from considering credible data alongside individual outcomes. For those exploring red light therapy, this means tuning into your body's response while staying open to new scientific developments. Adapting your approach based on emerging evidence supports informed, goal-oriented health choices.

Stories from real users showcase how red light therapy can make a meaningful difference in everyday life. One individual found that regular sessions helped ease the weight of seasonal depression, turning winter into a time of growth instead of gloom. Another shared how consistent use led to fewer migraines and milder symptoms when they did occur. These accounts may differ in detail, but they share a common theme: the therapy's ability to support well-being in diverse, personalized ways.

It is crucial to approach red light therapy with a mindset of discovery and without pre-set expectations. Its effects vary depending on personal conditions and usage protocols. Some may experience swift benefits, while others notice gradual advancements. Patient perseverance is fundamental; maintaining steady effort guarantees the most rewarding outcomes.

Monitoring progress offers valuable insights into how red light therapy affects you individually. Keeping a journal or using a tracking app can help document sessions, symptom changes, or overall well-being. This practice enhances accountability and provides a concrete record of your therapy journey. It also helps tailor expectations and adjustments according to genuine observations over time.

Manufacturers of some red light therapy units have developed several apps that you can use to track your sessions and results. I have also included a tracking guide in the back of the book that you can use, and a downloadable tracking journal is provided for free with the purchase of this book.

Addressing Safety Concerns: Dispelling Fears

It's completely understandable to question the safety of any health technology you're considering. Openly addressing these concerns helps build confidence. A common worry with red light therapy is whether it can harm the skin. As mentioned earlier, red light therapy is often confused with UV light, the latter which is known for causing sunburn and accelerating aging. However, red light operates very differently. It's a non-ionizing form of light, meaning it cannot damage DNA or harm skin cells. Instead, it penetrates gently to support healing and regeneration without the risks associated with UV exposure. You can feel confident knowing that red light therapy is safe for your skin.

Eye safety is another prevalent worry. Our instincts urge us to shield our eyes from bright lights. Direct exposure to intense light can indeed be uncomfortable or harmful over time. Thankfully, red light therapy devices are equipped with safety in mind. During sessions, protective eyewear is advised to circumvent any potential discomfort from lighting exposure. These glasses are similar to sunglasses, mitigating glare and ensuring your eyes remain at ease throughout the treatment. Incorporating this precaution allows you to enjoy the benefits without endangering your vision.

Getting the most out of red light therapy means using it wisely. While it is tempting to think that longer sessions lead to faster results, overuse can cause discomfort or fatigue.

That's why following the session times recommended by your device's manufacturer is important. These guidelines are designed to keep your experience safe, comfortable, and effective.

Sensitivity varies among individuals. Some may have heightened skin sensitivity and feel slight warming during sessions. If this applies, begin with shorter sessions, slowly increasing the time as your body acclimates. This approach ensures comfortable adaptation while maximizing benefits and minimizing irritation.

Dermatologists advocate red light therapy for its safety and noninvasive nature, making it a compatible addition to skincare routines. Consulting healthcare professionals before starting is advisable, particularly if you have health conditions or medications that could be affected. This precaution ensures the therapy aligns with your health profile, instilling confidence that you are making the right choice.

Feedback from certified practitioners also strengthens confidence. These experts stress the importance of procuring high-quality devices from reputable producers, highlighting the benefits of consistent performance and adherence to safety standards.

One practical piece of professional advice is to craft a dedicated therapy space at home where you can relax and focus solely on your therapy sessions. Creating a serene environment free from distractions encourages relaxation and focus, which can significantly enhance the experience. This builds a mental association between the therapy and peace, enhancing its psychological benefits and helping you establish a consistent routine.

When you understand the safety of red light therapy, it's easier to see it for what it truly is—a gentle, supportive tool that helps you feel your best. Using it mindfully and consistently creates a safe space for healing and self-care. Each session is more than just a treatment—it's a step toward the vibrant, healthy life you're building.

Realistic Expectations: Understanding Therapy Outcomes

Taking the first step in a new health practice often brings both excitement and uncertainty. With red light therapy, it's helpful to remember that meaningful results take time. This isn't a quick fix—it's a tool that works with your body to promote gradual, lasting change. Like tending to a garden, consistent care and patience lead to growth and visible transformation over time.

Each individual's experience with red light therapy is distinct. While some observe progress quickly, others witness subtle shifts over time. This variance is typical, contingent on factors such as your health's current state and your body's response to therapy. Those addressing inflammation may see swift relief compared to individuals focused on skin renewal.

Achieving meaningful results with red light therapy requires both patience and consistency. Like physical exercise, its effectiveness is closely linked to regular practice. Skipping sessions or extending breaks can disrupt progress, while staying committed allows benefits to build over time. It's also important to consider individual health needs; for example, chronic conditions such as pain or skin disorders may require longer use compared to general wellness goals. Finding a consistent rhythm that fits your lifestyle is key to long-term success.

Real-life stories bring the power of red light therapy to life. John found significant relief from joint pain after sticking with regular sessions, while Lisa noticed a slow but steady improvement in her skin's appearance. Her experience reminds us that results don't always happen overnight, but they *do* happen. Whether big or small, each outcome speaks to the different ways this therapy can make a positive difference.

Treat patience as a key element of your therapeutic process. Tracking your progress provides motivation and insight into individual experiences. Maintaining a journal or photographing regular updates helps unveil changes that might escape daily notice. This personal archive keeps you engaged with the process, allowing expectations to evolve realistically based on tangible evidence.

As your wellness journey unfolds, your goals may naturally change—and that's part of the process. What once felt like a specific aim may become a broader commitment to feeling your best. By embracing each phase of progress, whether big or small, you give yourself space to grow, heal, and thrive in your own way.

Viewing red light therapy as a partnership between you and your body is essential. It requires consistency, and in return, it delivers steady, visible benefits. When you embrace its gradual nature, you create space for long-term success. Armed with knowledge and realistic expectations, you can confidently incorporate this therapy into your routine—not just for physical improvements but as a meaningful part of your overall wellness journey.

Chapter 3

THE TOOLS OF THE TRADE

Red and near-infrared light improves mitochondrial function, which is central to almost all bodily healing processes.

–DR. JOSEPH MERCOLA

Choosing Your Device: A Comprehensive Guide

EXPLORING RED LIGHT THERAPY starts with one crucial question: Which device is right for you? With so many options available, finding the best fit can be challenging, but this crucial step will shape your results. Whether your focus is skin health, pain relief, or full-body wellness, understanding what to look for makes all the difference. Let's look at the essential features to guide your decision and highlight a few details you might not have considered.

Wavelength is key when selecting a red light therapy device, as each range targets different treatment goals. Red light wavelengths between 630 and 660 nanometers are best suited for skin-related concerns because they stimulate collagen, improve texture, and promote a youthful glow. For therapy targeting muscle recovery or joint discomfort, near-infrared wavelengths between 810 and 850 nanometers are more effective due to their deeper tissue penetration. Aligning the device's wavelength with your specific needs is essential for achieving optimal therapeutic outcomes.

Further, consider the device's size relative to your treatment scope. Are you seeking full-body exposure or localized therapy, such as facial treatments or joint-specific relief? Panel devices, offering extensive coverage, can be mounted or strategically placed for convenient, effortless therapy sessions. They are ideal for comprehensive treatment needs, enveloping the body in a cocoon of healing light.

Handheld devices provide precision, which allows you to intensely focus on isolated areas or problem spots. Wearable devices provide ease and adaptability, seamlessly integrating therapy into an active lifestyle while catering to diverse preferences.

Portability matters if you're always on the move or working with limited space, which is another reason handheld and wearable red light therapy devices are so helpful—they're easy to use, effective, and perfect for multitasking. You could use one while sipping your morning coffee or winding down in the evening. These compact tools bring you wellness wherever you are, making it easier than ever to stay consistent without rearranging your entire day.

Budget and financial considerations are equally crucial. Balance cost, quality, and efficacy to ensure your investment aligns with financial boundaries and therapeutic needs. Conducting a cost-benefit analysis can be enlightening, helping demystify the choice between premium and lower-priced models. While premium devices might dazzle with advanced features and a higher power output, more budget-friendly options also deliver substantial gains when used diligently.

Red light therapy is an investment in health, promising wellness returns and enhanced vitality. So, choose wisely to align with your personal values and health aspirations.

User testimonials and expert evaluations offer invaluable insights into device reliability and efficacy. On reputable review platforms, users often detail ease of use, durability, and treatment effectiveness. Health professionals, on the other hand, are well-versed in the nuances of red light therapy, so they can recommend devices that target unique health objectives. Gleaning advice from multiple sources ensures a well-rounded perspective, helping you make educated decisions. Below is a sample chart of various suppliers of red light therapy and the particulars of what wavelength you need for the condition you want to address. More and more options are becoming available as this therapy continues to gain in popularity. Also included are some average price points so you can plan around your budget.

Top Red Light Therapy Devices

Device	Best For	Wavelengths (nm)	Average Price
Omnilux Contour FACE	Skin rejuvenation, anti-aging, acne	633 (red), 830 (near-infrared)	$395
Dr. Dennis Gross SpectraLite FaceWare Pro	Wrinkles, acne, collagen stimulation	630 (red), 415 (blue)	$455
Celluma PRO	Pain relief, skin repair, inflammation, acne	630 (red), 880 (near-infrared)	$1,795
MitoPOD™	Full-body wellness, immune support, pain relief	660 (red), 850 (near-infrared)	$3,995
Solawave 4-in-1 Wand	Spot treatments, facial toning, anti-aging	660 (red)	$149
TheraFace PRO	Facial massage, skin firming, relaxation	660 (red), 850 (near-infrared)	$399
Body Balance OvationULT Bed	Full-body therapy for pain, inflammation, immune support	660 (red), 850 (near-infrared)	$50,000
LightStim for Pain and Anti-Aging	Pain relief, anti-aging, skin tone improvement	605 (amber), 630 (red), 660 (deep red), 855 (infrared)	$249–$449

Wavelengths by Condition

Condition	Recommended Wavelengths (nm)	Notes
Skin Repair	630–660 (red)	Stimulates collagen production and enhances skin tone and texture
Pain Relief	810–880 (near-infrared)	Penetrates deep into tissues to reduce inflammation and alleviate pain
Mental Focus	810–850 (near-infrared)	Enhances cerebral blood flow and supports cognitive function
Depression & Anxiety	810–850 (near-infrared)	Modulates physiological processes to improve mood and reduce anxiety
Immune Support	660–850 (red and near-infrared)	Boosts cellular energy production and supports immune system function

Red Light Therapy Device Price Ranges

Device Type	Price Range
Facial Masks & Wands	$150–$500
Mid-Size Panels & Belts	$800–$2,000
Full-Body Systems	$3,000–$50,000

Pro Tip: Choose a dual-wavelength device (e.g., 660 nm + 850 nm) to experience both skin-enhancing and deep-healing effects in a single session.

The above checklist provides a detailed comparison of different wavelength options depending on the therapy desired. This tool streamlines your decision-making, ensuring your choice is well-suited to health and lifestyle expectations.

How the red light therapy device personally resonates with you is equally important. Each device offers unique features for improved skin health, pain relief, or holistic wellness. The appropriate device is a powerful partner in your well-being adventure, facilitating a transformative experience tailored to your personal health narrative.

The spectrum of possibilities within red light therapy provides tools to meet varied preferences and needs. Understanding key factors in device selection and leveraging reliable resources empowers you to make educated choices, elevating your therapy experience. Continue this exploration to maximize red light therapy's potential for a brighter, healthier life.

LEDs and Lasers: Understanding Device Specifications

Understanding whether to select lasers or light-emitting diodes (LEDs) for your red light therapy device is essential, as each offers distinct benefits. Lasers, renowned for their precision, provide focused, monochromatic beams ideal for meticulously targeted treatments. The coherence of laser light enables deep penetration that can effectively treat precise, localized conditions, aiding in focused healing modalities that boost recovery.

In contrast, LEDs cast a broader, diffused light, making them preferable for expansive coverage. Although this diffusion doesn't reach the same depths as lasers, it effectively treats surface-level issues over larger areas, ideal for comprehensive skin treatments or broad wellness applications. LED therapy's mild, encompassing nature provides a gentle yet effective approach for overall wellness. Both device types boast strengths, and your choice hinges on the specific therapeutic needs you aim to address.

Power output matters when selecting a red light therapy device. The power output for red light therapy devices, measured in joules per square centimeter (J/cm^2), determines how much energy is delivered during a session. Higher output means shorter treatment times, making powerful devices more efficient. Lower-output models may still be effective but require longer sessions to achieve similar results.

Wavelengths play a pivotal role in the effectiveness of red light therapy, each offering unique healing properties. Near-infrared light reaches deep into the body, targeting muscles and joints for relief and recovery at the structural level. Red light gently nourishes the skin, promoting collagen synthesis and supporting a radiant, revitalized complexion. Choosing the right wavelength ensures a more intentional and personalized wellness experience.

Understanding technical specifications, often laden with terminology like irradiance and energy density, boosts your therapy's effectiveness. Irradiance describes power received per area (in milliwatts per square centimeter), influencing light energy skin absorption during sessions. Higher irradiance ensures quicker energy delivery, positively impacting treatment success.

Think of energy density as the amount of energy delivered to a particular area over time—it's a key factor in finding the correct device for your needs and lifestyle. By understanding these terms, you can make confident choices and shape a therapy routine that supports your health and wellness goals.

Technical Specification Glossary

When you begin looking for the device that best fits your needs, you might run into some technical or medical jargon that's new to you. Don't worry—below is a simple guide to the key terms you're likely to see, along with what they mean.

Glossary of Red Light Therapy Terms

Term	Definition
Red Light Therapy (RLT)	A technique using red and near-infrared light to promote healing and cellular function
Wavelength	The distance between light waves, measured in nanometers (nm); determines depth of tissue penetration
Photobiomodulation (PBM)	Scientific term for light therapy's effect on cells, enhancing healing and reducing inflammation
Chromophore	A molecule that absorbs light; cytochrome c oxidase in mitochondria is key in RLT
Mitochondria	The "powerhouse" of the cell that produces energy (ATP); stimulated by RLT
ATP (Adenosine Triphosphate)	Main energy molecule in cells; increased through RLT
Irradiance	Light power per area (mW/cm²); measures intensity of RLT exposure
Dosage / Fluence	Total energy delivered (J/cm²); calculated as irradiance × time
LED (Light Emitting Diode)	Common RLT light source; emits specific therapeutic wavelengths
Penetration Depth	How deeply light travels into tissues; longer wavelengths penetrate deeper
Reactive Oxygen Species (ROS)	Molecules that signal healing when produced in moderation by RLT
Cellular Regeneration	Replacement of damaged cells with healthy ones; enhanced by RLT
Nitric Oxide (NO)	A molecule released by RLT that improves blood flow through vasodilation
Inflammatory Response	The body's reaction to injury; RLT helps reduce excessive inflammation
Thermal vs. Nonthermal	RLT is nonthermal—benefits come from light, not heat
Photorejuvenation	Skin renewal using light to reduce wrinkles and boost collagen

Red light therapy devices aren't one-size-fits-all—each caters to different goals and styles. Whether you're drawn to the targeted power of lasers or the broader coverage of LEDs, knowing the difference helps you explore what works best for your wellness path.

As you explore the details behind device specifications, you will see how technology shapes today's health practices. Understanding these elements transforms red light therapy from a simple routine into a mindful, informed self-care practice. With this knowledge, you can confidently and clearly navigate your therapy choices, supporting your wellness journey.

Safety First: Precautions and Best Practices

Safety takes precedence in red light therapy, ensuring optimal session outcomes while safeguarding well-being. Eye protection is critical; although the light is non-UV, it can still cause discomfort. Protective goggles significantly enhance safety, enabling uninterrupted, relaxed engagement with therapy.

Attention to skin sensitivity is wise. Testing a small skin patch before comprehensive sessions helps avert unexpected reactions. A brief, controlled light application gauges skin tolerance. If irritation is absent, proceed confidently; otherwise, adjust parameters or consult healthcare professionals. This precaution exemplifies prudent, considerate practice.

Despite its general safety, red light therapy isn't universally suitable. Individuals with photosensitivity disorders or medications increasing light sensitivity require cautious approaches. Consulting healthcare professionals before initiating therapy is prudent, especially with existing health conditions or during pregnancy. Expert guidance personalizes experiences, providing reassurance and tailored advice.

Adhering closely to manufacturer instructions is critical. Device-specific guidelines underline safe operation aspects like distancing, session length, and device parameters. Disregarding these could lead to subpar outcomes or discomfort. Understanding these guides enhances device efficacy and user safety.

Implementing a pre-session checklist is advisable. Verify protective eyewear, ensure correct device placement, and clear hazards to create a secure environment. Post-session, care for your device by unplugging it, storing it safely, and inspecting it regularly for wear. Handling potential issues early averts larger complications, promoting sustained efficacy.

Safety Checklist

Red Light Therapy Safety Checklist

Safety Step	Details
☑ Read the user manual	Follow the manufacturer's instructions for setup, duration, and distance.
☑ Check device certification	Ensure the device is FDA-cleared or medically certified for home use.
☑ Start with short sessions	Begin with 5–10 minutes and gradually increase based on comfort and results.
☑ Maintain proper distance	Position yourself at the recommended distance (usually 6–12 inches).
☑ Avoid overuse	Stick to the recommended frequency (e.g., 3–5 times per week).
☑ Protect eyes if needed	Use goggles or keep eyes closed if light is intense near the face.
☑ Keep skin clean	Clean skin before use to avoid interference from lotions or makeup.
☑ Monitor skin response	Discontinue use if you notice irritation, redness, or discomfort.
☑ Stay hydrated	Drink water before and after sessions to support cellular function.
☑ Ensure ventilation	Use in a well-ventilated area to avoid overheating.
☑ Check device temperature	Allow device to cool between sessions if it becomes too warm.
☑ Avoid use on open wounds	Unless specified safe, avoid applying light directly to open or infected areas.
☑ Consult a professional (if needed)	Speak with a healthcare provider if you have medical conditions or concerns.

Although red light therapy offers significant benefits, it doesn't replace medical treatment. Consultations remain crucial for persistent issues, delivering insightful integration within broader health plans.

Red light therapy's natural advantages unfold safely when best practices are observed. Prioritizing safety and following guidelines lead to rewarding therapy experiences. Precautions ensure therapy remains effective and enjoyable, whether for skin rejuvenation, pain relief, or energy enhancement.

As you delve deeper into red light therapy, consider these safety tips as routine staples. These guidelines foster successful sessions, enriching your health journey toward a healthier future where efficacy meets safety to illuminate wellness paths.

Setting Up for Success: Creating Your Home Therapy Zone

A thoughtfully arranged space for red light therapy at home can turn your wellness routine into a truly restorative experience. Select a calm and private area—a bedroom nook or a cozy living room space—where you can retreat with ease. Limiting distractions will help you stay present and connected to the process. Let fresh air circulate through the space and soften the lighting around you to foster a tranquil, healing atmosphere.

Outfitting your therapy area with the right elements can make your sessions more enjoyable and effective. Choose a comfortable seat that invites relaxation—a soft chair or recliner works well. Adjustable stands help you properly align your device to stay comfortable and avoid unnecessary strain. Limited on space? No problem. A folding chair and wall-mounted unit can offer a simple, space-saving setup that still supports your wellness goals.

Keeping your setup efficient and easy to use makes all the difference. Try using furniture that doubles as storage or installing shelves to keep everything tidy and within reach. Arrange your device so it feels comfortable on your body. This leads to better results and makes your therapy feel like a natural part of your day.

After all, sticking with therapy is much easier when it becomes part of your everyday habits. Routines help anchor it into your life—whether a short session before work or a calming practice before bed, consistency brings results.

You don't need to overhaul your schedule to make it work. Ten quiet minutes during morning coffee or as part of your evening self-care—like reading or meditating—can make therapy feel like a comforting routine instead of something extra.

When you keep your routine consistent, your therapy spot can become a cozy escape from the everyday grind. Putting some thought into making it your own—comfortable and calming—can really boost the quality of your sessions. And the best part? That peaceful vibe can stay with you long after the therapy ends, supporting your overall wellness.

Remember, this space is yours to design, reflecting personal preferences and unleashing light therapy's healing potential. Adapt setups over time to accommodate routine alterations or personal preferences, supporting relaxation and rejuvenation and unlocking red light therapy's potential from home.

Maintenance and Care: Keeping Your Device in Top Shape

Maintaining your red light therapy device is like caring for a cherished asset, ensuring continued efficacy and reliability. Start with routine cleaning. Dust on lenses or device surfaces can reduce light efficiency. Use a soft, lint-free cloth to wipe down your device, keeping it clean and preventing smudges. For devices with detachable lenses, adhere to manufacturer instructions for cleaning to avoid scratches.

Proactively examine wear and tear. Regular inspections reveal potential damage or malfunctions. Loose connections or frayed cords pose performance or safety risks. Identifying issues early prevents larger problems. Watch for signs like flickering lights or inconsistent output, which may signal servicing or expert inspection needs.

Troubleshooting common issues often involves straightforward solutions. Verify power connections and outlet functions if a device won't turn on. Check circuit breakers or replace blown fuses if needed. Overheating concerns may arise when devices operate continuously without breaks. Cooling intervals between sessions prolong device life and maintain efficacy.

Proper storage and handling also contribute significantly to device longevity. Store your device safely, away from temperature extremes or moisture, which can cause internal damage. A cushioned case or designated storage box offers protection against bumps or accidental falls. Ensure secure packing during travel to prevent transport jostling, preserving device integrity for future use.

Regular functionality checks ensure devices operate correctly. Test performance by observing light output and consistency. Significant performance deviations prompt manufacturer consultation for maintenance or part replacement. Many manufacturers offer servicing options or replacement parts to sustain device longevity and effective therapy delivery.

In essence, device care is balancing routine maintenance with diligent usage. Implementing these simple practices and following guidelines sustains device quality, extends device life, and ensures consistent and effective therapy sessions. A proactive maintenance approach, over time, will promise peace of mind from your wellness investment.

As we explore further, device upkeep forms just one piece of the wellness puzzle. Future chapters will delve deeper into maximizing the benefits of red light therapy, ensuring insights align with your health aspirations. Together, we'll move toward heightened vitality and health—one enlightening therapy session at a time.

Chapter 4

INTEGRATING THERAPY INTO DAILY LIFE

A daily dose of red light is like sunshine for your skin—without the burn.

–UNKNOWN

Time Management: Scheduling Your Therapy Sessions

YOUR DAILY LIFE IS like a current of moments, duties, and connections. At first glance, incorporating red light therapy into this flow may feel overwhelming. But by creating a routine that aligns with your personal pace, you can naturally integrate it. Take time to assess what fills your day. Whether it's work deadlines, family responsibilities, or cherished personal rituals, each part of your day holds space where therapy might gently find a place.

Maximizing Flexibility

A weekly planner can be a powerful tool for clarity. Write down all your commitments—big or small—to create a clear picture of your time. Within that layout, look for moments that lend themselves to stillness and self-care. Maybe you find peace in the early morning stillness, or perhaps a mid-afternoon break provides the perfect pause. Integrating therapy into your schedule doesn't mean adding pressure—it's about creating space with purpose. With mindfulness and planning, your therapy sessions can become a treasured part of your daily rhythm.

Consistency and Adaptability

Regularity in red light therapy sessions is paramount for cumulative benefits, akin to nurturing a sapling that flourishes with consistent care. Employ technological aids, such as setting alarms or using calendar applications, as gentle reminders within the hectic pace of your day. The sight of "Red Light Time" on your agenda can highlight your commitment to well-being. Consistency promises lasting wellness dividends, translating into tangible outcomes.

Life's unpredictability, however, can render any routine challenging. Unforeseen responsibilities or emergencies might disrupt even the best-laid plans. In such scenarios, adaptability becomes your ally. Should unanticipated events arise, consider postponing your session to an alternate slot within the day. Red light therapy's flexibility allows you to navigate setbacks without derailing your health objectives.

Harnessing Technology

Embracing modern tech tools can simplify therapy integration. Calendar apps and digital planners provide functionalities that enable easy adjustments to your schedule. The ability to shuffle sessions around as life necessitates maintains an agile routine that prioritizes health amidst a chaotic lifestyle.

Visual Element: Weekly Planning Template

A weekly planning template can be an effective visual aid in this integration process. Visualizing therapy's placement within your schedule facilitates a balanced and consistent wellness approach.

Including moments of post-therapy reflection can deepen integration. Spend a few moments jotting down physical sensations or mental shifts observed after a session. This exercise fine-tunes your schedule and enriches your understanding of therapy's impact, fortifying the rationale for integrating red light therapy into daily life.

By crafting such schedules thoughtfully, red light therapy transforms a mundane task into an integral aspect of wellness. Persistent adjustments and reflections optimize efficacy, enriching your sense of fulfillment and balance.

Morning Rituals: Starting Your Day With Red Light

Start your morning wrapped in the glow of red light therapy, inviting peace and a sense of renewal. As the warm light fills your space, it awakens not just your body but also your inner drive. This soothing ritual can uplift your mood, boost clarity, and energize your day from the very first moments—like gently switching your mind from rest to readiness, fully prepared for whatever lies ahead.

Combining Practices

Pairing red light therapy with morning meditation can set a strong foundation for the day. Visualize sitting comfortably as the red light envelops you, eyes closed, with deep breaths synchronizing mind and body. This peaceful initiation amplifies the benefits of both practices, anchoring you before the day's cacophony ensues. Another integration method involves harmonizing therapy with your skincare ritual. As you apply nourishing creams or serums, let the warm light enhance rejuvenation, working beneath your skin's surface.

Morning exposure to red light offers powerful physiological benefits. Research highlights its ability to enhance alertness and mental clarity, helping you approach daily tasks more efficiently. It illuminates the corners of your mind, unlocking focus and uplifting your mood. This gentle boost can set the tone for a productive, energized day—where your outer glow mirrors your inner vitality.

Creating Your Morning Zen

A dedicated morning therapy space can set the tone for a revitalizing day. Find a cozy corner where the red light can mingle with natural sunlight, creating a warm, soothing atmosphere. Start with five quiet minutes of stillness or breathwork beneath the glow, flowing naturally into your skincare or reflective practices. Most people find 10–15 minutes ideal, but your routine can be tailored to what feels best for you as your practice evolves.

Real-Life Transformations

Professionals leading busy lives often find that red light therapy endows them with a competitive edge. Consider the executive who shared how morning sessions optimized her focus during high-pressure meetings, significantly enhancing her performance. Likewise, an avid runner swears by his morning red light ritual, which preps his muscles for jogs by dissolving stiffness and boosting endurance.

Such testimonials reveal that morning routines extend beyond physical health—they embody holistic self-care amidst busy lives. These narratives illustrate how minor adjustments can yield substantial lifestyle improvements. Dedication of just a few moments each morning primes the mind and body for the day's challenges and highlights.

To begin your red light journey, you must discover what resonates uniquely with you. Experiment with various practices and timings, embracing what truly aligns. Each session symbolizes a new awakening—a recharge before engaging in the day's demands.

Ultimately, incorporating red light therapy into your morning isn't merely adding another task to your checklist. Instead, it signifies your commitment to adopting a deeper self-connection, greeting each day with light and life. Each session fortifies your health, nurturing an inner vigor that endures through the challenges lying ahead.

Evening Wind-Down: Relaxing and Rejuvenating Before Bed

As evening settles in, consider transforming your nightly routine into a sanctuary of peace with the help of red light therapy. Let the gentle glow of your device wash over your space, signaling your body that it's time to wind down. Combine this calming light with deep breathing or progressive muscle relaxation to release the day's tension. To deepen the experience, add soft music or nature sounds—like rustling leaves or gentle waves—to turn your session into a relaxing escape within your home.

Sleep Enhancement

Red light therapy possesses remarkable efficacy in enhancing sleep quality when used in evening routines. It aids in regulating melatonin production—a hormone that prompts the body into resting mode. This effectiveness is especially beneficial for those grappling with sleep disturbances, facilitating a smoother transition into slumber and resulting in a rejuvenated awakening. Beyond sleep, nighttime therapy alleviates built-up stress and tension, fostering deep relaxation conducive to restful sleep.

Creating Your Retreat

Crafting a restorative evening routine involves arranging the therapy setting for optimal relaxation. Dim the lights in your sanctuary to cast the space in tranquility. A clutter-free area clears the mind and reinforces the intentionality of this time dedicated to pure relaxation. Sessions lasting 10–20 minutes strike a good balance, providing unwinding benefits without any overstimulation before bed. Let each deep breath anchor deeper calmness as you ease into your session's tranquility.

Enhancing Calming Effects

To enhance the soothing impact of red light therapy, add calming rituals to your evening routine. Aromatherapy with lavender or chamomile can create a peaceful atmosphere, especially when used in a diffuser or as a pillow mist. Gentle stretching after your session can help your muscles relax and your mind unwind, making it easier to release the day's stress.

Reflection Section

Occasionally pause to reflect on how these evening practices enhance your tranquility and sleep quality. Maintaining a journal documenting experiences pre- and post-therapy yields insightful reflections, aiding in refining and adapting routines more effectively.

Evening red light therapy creates ripe opportunities for reflection and growth. Bathed in comforting light, take a moment to ponder your day's achievements and challenges. This thoughtful introspection deepens gratitude and mindfulness, enriching your overall wellness journey.

The aim of these evening routines is twofold—cultivating relaxation and overall rejuvenation. Deliberately crafting this time for yourself creates a beneficial and treasured ritual. Remember, the core purpose is to shed daily burdens and embrace serenity.

Incorporating an evening routine centered around red light therapy nurtures physical relaxation and mental peace. It imparts a moment of tranquility amidst life's chaos and presents an opportunity to decelerate and reconnect. These practices offer a conduit toward enriched well-being, whether enhancing sleep or unwinding.

On-the-Go Solutions: Portable Devices for Busy Lives

With today's busy schedules, maintaining wellness can be a challenge, but red light therapy has kept pace. Compact devices make it easy to stay on track even when you're on the go, offering targeted support whether you're traveling, commuting, or working long hours. Small enough to fit in a pocket, these tools bring relief when and where it's needed. Wearable versions take it even further, as they can slip under clothes and deliver therapy quietly and effortlessly throughout your day.

Seamless Mobility

The allure of portable red light therapy lies in its seamless integration into daily life. For frequent travelers and busy commuters, portable red light therapy devices are a game changer. They allow you to transform downtime—whether in airports, during layovers, or on your daily commute—into moments of self-care. A quiet corner and a few minutes are all you need. Holding a device on the go means you don't have to pause your wellness journey just because you're in motion. With this flexibility, therapy becomes part of your everyday rhythm—wherever life takes you.

Portable devices dismantle these constraints, making them ideal for dynamic lifestyles. Frequent flyers laud their versatility and ability to transport therapy across bustling terminals to tranquil havens. One seasoned traveler claims that handheld devices alleviated jet lag, optimizing energy and productivity at international conferences. Office workers capitalize on brief lunch breaks for rejuvenation before facing the afternoon rigor. Those with active lifestyles share similar stories. Fitness enthusiasts treasure these devices for their post-workout recovery and muscle relaxation benefits during cool-downs. One marathoner credited a wearable accessory with hastening recovery and maintaining uninterrupted training momentum. The convenience of having therapy in your pocket guarantees unwavering health dedication without impeding existing commitments.

As technology advances, anticipate enhanced efficiency and user-friendliness, which has the potential to eradicate additional holistic health barriers. Whether in an office cubicle, mid-flight, or comfortably at home, wellness routines adapt with ease and accessibility.

Tracking Progress: Monitoring Results and Adjustments

Starting your red light therapy journey is an exciting step toward improved well-being. But how can you tell if it's actually working for you? The answer may lie in tracking your progress. Keeping a simple record of your sessions can help you recognize what's effective, making it easier to adjust your routine for maximum benefit. Think of it as your personal guide, helping you spot patterns, celebrate milestones, and make wise, wellness-driven choices.

Tracking progress can be seamlessly achieved through journaling. Whether via the attached downloadable tracking journal, a traditional notebook, or a digital alternative, recording details helps build self-awareness. Note each session's specifics—date, time, duration, and targeted focal areas. More importantly, document related symptoms or condition shifts. Has your skin acquired newfound smoothness? Have muscle aches dissipated? Exploring these patterns yields invaluable data reflecting therapy's actual contributions.

Tools like tracking templates or self-assessment questionnaires can be incredibly useful to boost the effectiveness of your red light therapy practice. They make it easier to monitor progress and evaluate results over time. These resources might include symptom rating scales, notes on energy levels, or reflections on mood changes. As your entries accumulate, they offer a clear picture of your journey, helping you see the true impact of the therapy.

Adaptive Strategy

Analyzing compiled data unveils significant insights, enabling therapy plans to be recalibrated for enhanced results. Maybe longer sessions generate superior outcomes, or focusing on one specific area provides meaningful relief. These revelations facilitate mindful optimization, allowing you to adjust session parameters to extract full potential while ensuring persisting progress.

Success stories abound among those systematically documenting their red light therapy journey. Consider Sarah, burdened with chronic joint pain, who meticulously tracked sessions and recognized efficacy in shorter, frequent intervals, significantly lessening discomfort. Her experience epitomizes empowerment derived from systematic tracking and personalized adjustments.

A different narrative is Tom's, who integrated red light therapy for improved sleep quality. Through methodically documenting evening routines and subsequent restfulness, he discerned that timing adjustments yielded the most significant sleep improvements. This minor tweak greatly influenced holistic wellness, underscoring the importance of tracking for meeting personal health objectives.

Reflection and Growth

Reflection significantly enriches the tracking process. Set weekly intervals for progress reviews. Reflect on any observed advancements and explore further refinement opportunities. Such practices foster a deeper resonance with your health optimization journey, bolstering positive habits and sustained dedication.

Ultimately, when you embrace tracking, you are actively participating in your wellness trajectory. By tuning into your body's responses and making informed decisions, therapy becomes organically personalized. As you review logs and evaluate patterns, you're not just observing changes but orchestrating them.

As this chapter concludes, recognize that tracking is more than a tool—it's part of a transformative mindset redefining red light therapy perceptions. Within this framework, you're poised for triumph and lay the foundation for future health achievements. With your newfound insights, proceed to the next chapter, where you'll discover novel strategies and enlightening techniques that can further enrich your life.

Chapter 5

TARGETED APPLICATIONS AND TECHNIQUES

Low-level light therapy has been shown to reduce inflammation and promote wound healing.

–JOURNAL OF PHOTOCHEMISTRY AND PHOTOBIOLOGY

Pain Management: Relieving Chronic Discomfort

WAKING UP EACH MORNING with stiff, aching joints is a daily struggle for many living with chronic pain, but red light therapy presents a promising solution for relief. By targeting inflammation at the cellular level, this therapy helps ease discomfort through several biological processes. One important mechanism involves suppressing prostaglandin synthesis, compounds known to trigger inflammation and pain. By inhibiting their production, red light therapy can help reduce the symptoms commonly associated with inflammatory conditions.

However, this therapy does more than reduce inflammation. It stimulates the release of endorphins, our body's natural painkillers. Visualize these endorphins as tiny warriors rushing to the site of discomfort, easing pain from within. This dual action—reducing inflammation and boosting endorphin levels—creates a powerful synergy that can alleviate chronic pain without the reliance on pharmaceuticals. The potential for reduced medication usage is particularly appealing to those concerned about side effects and dependency.

Specific techniques are crucial when utilizing this therapy for optimal pain relief. Positioning a red light therapy device close to the affected area is essential to address joint and muscle pain. Start by sitting or lying comfortably, ensuring the light reaches the target spot directly. Individuals often find significant improvements through daily sessions of 10–20 minutes. For smaller areas like wrists or knees, using localized devices allows for precision and optimized results.

It's helpful to understand how your device works to get the most out of your sessions. Red light in the 600–650 nm range reaches deeper tissues and encourages cellular healing. Alongside the right wavelength, consistent daily therapy time can help your body gradually adjust and amplify the benefits you experience over time.

Numerous real-life stories reflect the effectiveness of red light therapy. For instance, arthritis patients have experienced remarkable improvements in joint mobility and pain reduction after regular sessions. Jane, for example, shared how she could resume tending to her garden, an activity she had abandoned due to arthritis pain. Similarly, individuals with fibromyalgia have reported decreased widespread pain and stiffness, enabling them to adopt more active lifestyles with newfound enthusiasm.

Besides its standalone benefits, red light therapy effectively complements other treatments. Pairing it with physical therapy can amplify results, as both techniques aim to enhance mobility and reduce discomfort. Physical therapists often integrate red light therapy before exercises to warm up muscles and joints, leading to faster recovery and improved outcomes.

Red light therapy doesn't have to replace pain medications; however, it can enhance their benefits. While medications may offer fast relief, red light therapy works at a deeper level, helping to reduce inflammation and support lasting healing. It's important to work with a healthcare professional to create a personalized plan that safely blends both approaches.

Mary's story is a powerful example. After years of struggling with chronic back pain, she decided to combine red light therapy with her prescribed treatments. Over time, she required less medication and felt more empowered in her daily life. The therapy helped her reconnect with activities she once avoided, giving her a renewed vitality.

Case Study: John's Journey to Pain Relief

Daily life had become difficult for John, a retiree whose arthritis made simple tasks like holding a pen or twisting a jar lid impossible. Things slowly changed once he began using red light therapy for 15 minutes a day on his hands. Month by month, he regained control and mobility in his fingers. Eventually, he could return to playing the piano—an old passion that once again filled his days with joy and purpose.

The experiences shared here reveal how powerful red light therapy can be when used regularly and with purpose. By zeroing in on areas of chronic pain and pairing therapy with other supportive strategies, many people are finding new freedom from discomfort. Whether you're managing arthritis, fibromyalgia, or something else, this approach can help you reconnect with the things you love—the hobbies, movement, and moments that pain once limited or stopped altogether.

Athletic Recovery: Enhancing Performance and Healing

Athletes constantly look for effective ways to push limits and recover faster. Red light therapy is quickly earning recognition as a powerful recovery aid. After demanding workouts, the warm, restorative light helps soothe tired muscles and jump-start the recovery process, getting you back in motion with less downtime.

This therapy reduces muscle soreness and accelerates post-exercise recovery, making it an ideal companion for athletes. The light penetrates deep into muscle tissues, promoting increased blood flow and reducing lactic acid buildup, a notorious culprit behind that lingering ache. Enhancing oxygen delivery to the muscles facilitates the clearance of metabolic waste, thus accelerating healing and reducing downtime between sessions.

Incorporating red light therapy into your fitness routine doesn't have to be complicated. Consistent use and smart timing make all the difference. A few minutes before a workout can warm up muscles, improve flexibility, and help prevent injuries. After training, spending 15–20 minutes under the light can ease soreness and inflammation, giving your body the recovery support it needs to recharge and be ready for the next challenge.

Introducing this routine requires minimal equipment and effort, as portable red light devices are widely available and easily fit into gym bags. Many athletes find that integrating short sessions is as simple as applying muscle balms or stretching; together, these practices turn therapy into a routine element of preparation and recovery. This methodical approach ensures that the therapy becomes an integral part of conditioning programs with minimal disruption.

Athletes in diverse sports have shared how red light therapy has transformed their training. From football fields to marathon courses, professionals are embracing its recovery-boosting power. One marathoner shared that since adding red light therapy to his routine, he experienced less muscle fatigue and greater endurance, cutting minutes off his race times. Personal trainers are also on board. One well-known trainer reported that clients experienced quicker gains and fewer setbacks after incorporating the therapy into their routines.

The synergy of red light therapy with other recovery methods further amplifies its effectiveness. Consider pairing it with cryotherapy, which utilizes extreme cold to reduce inflammation and promote healing. While cryotherapy constricts blood vessels, thereby reducing swelling, red light therapy complements it by enhancing circulation once blood flow resumes. This supports more efficient nutrient delivery and waste removal. Together, they form a potent duo that augments recovery beyond the capabilities of each method alone.

Likewise, integrating red light therapy with massage therapy offers a comprehensive approach to muscle care. On its own, massage alleviates tension and improves flexibility. When combined with red light therapy, the benefits are magnified: Enhanced relaxation from massage is compounded by the soothing effects of light therapy. Many therapists now incorporate red light therapy into their sessions, using it before or after massages to maximize client outcomes and satisfaction.

Red light therapy presents an innovative edge for athletes looking to push boundaries safely and naturally. It doesn't just promote faster healing—it helps athletes perform at a higher level overall. Whether you're a weekend warrior or a professional athlete, integrating this therapy into your routine could be the key to achieving new heights in performance and recovery. Embracing these techniques sets you on a path toward reaching your fitness goals with less pain and more gain, creating a robust and forward-thinking approach to athletic health.

Red light therapy's role in athletic recovery is gaining momentum as more athletes experience its multitude of benefits firsthand. It's no longer merely an add-on—it has evolved into a vital component of comprehensive training regimens. As success stories continue to emerge, the sports world is taking note of this cutting-edge approach to performance enhancement. Whether used alone or in conjunction with other methodologies, this therapy stands out as a valuable tool for anyone committed to athletic success, representing a new frontier in sports recovery and achievement.

Skin Rejuvenation: Techniques for a Youthful Glow

Restoring a youthful look is a common skincare goal, and red light therapy delivers a scientifically backed approach to help achieve it. When light is directed at wrinkle-prone areas, it stimulates collagen production, promoting skin elasticity and smoothness. It also reaches deep into the skin to energize cells and enhance their natural repair cycle. With consistent sessions, the therapy can gradually reduce the appearance of fine lines, leaving your skin more radiant and revitalized.

But the benefits continue beyond this point. Red light therapy is effective in addressing age spots and pigmentation issues. These often result from sun exposure and aging, yet they need not be permanent fixtures. The therapy promotes cellular turnover by enhancing blood circulation to the skin layers. This helps fade pigmentation, even out skin tone, and promote a clearer complexion over time. It's akin to hitting the reset button for your skin, encouraging more efficient self-renewal.

Incorporating red light therapy into your skincare routine is easier than you might think. At-home devices are designed for comfort and convenience—you can use them while relaxing with a book or your favorite show. For those looking for stronger results, professional treatments at dermatology clinics offer advanced technology and expert care. Regular check-ins with a provider can help fine-tune your treatment plan to best suit your unique skin goals.

Enhancing Your Skincare Routine

What makes these results possible lies in the skin's cellular response. Red light therapy activates keratinocytes, the cells that build the top layer of your skin. Their faster turnover helps keep skin fresh, healthy, and protected from external damage. Improved blood circulation also plays a role, ensuring your skin receives the nutrients and oxygen it needs to stay vibrant and strong.

Red light therapy is widely praised by dermatologists and skincare specialists for its role in supporting skin health. Its gentle approach and low risk of side effects make it a preferred option over more aggressive treatments. Skincare professionals also note that it can boost the performance of topical products. When paired with antioxidant serums containing vitamin C or E, red light therapy helps shield the skin from free radicals and enhances the therapy's overall rejuvenating benefits.

Another great companion to red light therapy is a moisturizer with hyaluronic acid, a trusted ingredient for locking in hydration and maintaining a supple, dewy complexion. Using it immediately after your session helps trap moisture while your skin is most receptive. The therapy's revitalizing effects and the moisturizer's hydrating power can noticeably improve skin tone and texture.

Emily, a dedicated skincare enthusiast, turned to red light therapy after struggling with stubborn age spots on her cheeks. After several months of consistent use, she saw a noticeable decrease in pigmentation and a more radiant overall skin tone. Her dermatologist also advised incorporating a vitamin C serum into her routine, which helped accelerate her progress and provided added protection against future sun damage.

These insights showcase how red light therapy can become a beneficial addition to your skincare routine. Its ability to blend seamlessly with other skincare elements makes it versatile and easy to incorporate into existing routines. It goes beyond enhancing appearance—it boosts confidence by fortifying skin health and vitality. Whether you're tackling fine lines or pigmentation issues, red light therapy offers a promising solution for achieving the radiant skin you've always desired.

As you explore these methods and tips, remember that consistency is vital—regular sessions paired with complementary products can lead to remarkable transformations over time. Consider how red light therapy might fit into your skincare goals and routines. It offers a modern approach to obtaining that cherished, youthful glow, which reflects beauty and, more importantly, more intrinsic well-being.

Mental Clarity: Improving Focus and Mood

Starting your day with mental clarity and resilience is essential, and red light therapy can help you get there. It increases cerebral blood flow, which supports enhanced oxygen and nutrient delivery to the brain. This results in improved focus and cognitive performance. It also balances key neurotransmitters like serotonin and dopamine, which are vital for mood regulation. This dual action promotes sharper thinking and emotional well-being, helping to reduce symptoms of anxiety and depression.

For red light therapy to effectively enhance mental clarity, timing is important. Morning sessions, especially when paired with calming routines, can boost mood and cognitive function. A few quiet moments in a softly lit space can provide a refreshing sense of focus and calm that sets a positive tone for the day ahead. Alternatively, a midday session can serve as a powerful reset, helping you overcome the standard afternoon energy dip and restore concentration when it's most needed.

Numerous personal stories highlight the cognitive benefits of red light therapy. Lisa, a college student, found it difficult to concentrate during extended study periods. After integrating red light therapy into her routine, she experienced significant improvements in focus and information retention. Similarly, working professionals have reported reduced brain fog and heightened productivity. Roger, a project manager, shared that regular sessions helped him remain mentally sharp in high-stress meetings, enhancing both critical thinking and creativity.

Red light therapy is gaining recognition not only for cognitive support but also for its role in managing mood disorders. Its ability to help regulate neurotransmitters makes it a valuable companion to treatments like cognitive behavioral therapy (CBT). Integrating therapy with practices such as mindfulness can provide a double layer of support that soothes the body while grounding the mind.

Emily, a young professional with a history of anxiety, found comfort and improvement when she added red light therapy to her CBT sessions. The combination eased her symptoms and gave her a greater sense of peace and resilience in daily life.

> **Reflection Section: Your Red Light Therapy Experience**
> Take a moment to think about times when your focus or mood felt off balance. Where in your daily routine could red light therapy make a meaningful difference? Reflect on how incorporating strategic sessions might support your mental clarity and emotional well-being. Let these insights help shape a therapy routine that works for you.

Red light therapy's potential to enhance mental clarity and mood presents an exciting area for exploration. Whether you're a student tackling exams or a professional managing workplace demands, this therapy has the potential to naturally optimize brain function. Its effects extend far beyond cognition, imbuing a sense of calm and balance that permeates every facet of life. As more individuals share their success stories, the possibilities seem boundless.

The beauty of red light therapy lies in its simplicity and accessibility. It doesn't require that you make abrupt changes overnight; instead, it will foster gradual improvements that accumulate over time. By embracing this practice and strategically integrating it into your routine, you open the door to enhanced mental acumen and emotional well-being.

In today's fast-paced world, discovering moments of calm and clarity is invaluable. Red light therapy offers such moments—a chance to pause, breathe deeply, and recalibrate. As you explore these techniques and stories, contemplate how this therapy might illuminate your path toward greater mental clarity and mood stability, ultimately contributing to a more balanced and enriched life.

Immune Support: Boosting Your Body's Defenses

A healthy immune system is your body's best line of defense, and red light therapy can help keep it strong. It activates lymphocytes, the immune cells responsible for recognizing and fighting threats. It also increases the production of macrophages, which target and eliminate harmful pathogens. These cellular boosts work together to create a more proactive, responsive immune system that helps you stay well and bounce back faster from everyday health challenges.

One approach to utilizing red light therapy for immune support is focusing on the frequency and duration of sessions. Regular sessions—two to three times per week—can fit into a wellness regimen alongside other practices like exercising and hydrating. This regimen is an invisible shield that reinforces the body's natural defenses and improves resilience against common pathogens prevalent in colder months.

Using red light therapy as part of your wellness routine during cold and flu season can be a preventative tool. Consistency is key, especially when sessions are directed at the lymph nodes—those vital immune hubs throughout your body. Stimulating these areas encourages better lymphatic drainage and circulation, helping your immune system stay alert and efficient in preventing illness.

Daily Immune-Boosting Practices

Clinical research supports the immune-enhancing potential of red light therapy. Studies have shown that individuals who engage in regular sessions report fewer instances of seasonal illness and recover more quickly when symptoms arise. Real-life experiences reinforce these findings. For example, Rhonda, who manages an autoimmune condition, noted a decrease in flare-ups and an improvement in her overall well-being after incorporating therapy into her daily routine.

Complementary lifestyle changes can further strengthen the immune system's response. Nutritional adjustments—such as increasing your intake of vitamins C and E through foods like citrus fruits, leafy greens, and nuts—supply essential nutrients that support immune health. Managing stress is equally important, as chronic stress impairs immune function. Incorporating yoga or meditation alongside red light therapy encourages relaxation and mental balance. These holistic strategies create a well-rounded approach to immune resilience and overall vitality.

Wrapping up this chapter on a hopeful note, remember that red light therapy can do wonders for your immune system—whether you're aiming to avoid seasonal bugs or manage ongoing health concerns. But this is just the beginning. In the pages ahead, we'll explore more ways this versatile therapy can enhance your everyday life. Stick with me as we uncover fresh ideas and easy-to-apply strategies for building a fulfilling, balanced lifestyle.

Make a Difference With Your Review

Unlock the Power of Generosity

"The best way to find yourself is to lose yourself in the service of others."

–MAHATMA GANDHI

Helping others brings a sense of joy that's hard to match. Would you join me in spreading that joy?

Imagine someone, just like you, who is looking for simple, practical ways to fight inflammation and aging, amplify energy, aid in weight loss, and support skin rejuvenation and cellular renewal. Your review could be the guiding light they need to begin their journey.

My goal with *Body Wisdom Through Red Light Therapy* is to make the tools for healing and connection easy and accessible for everyone. But to reach more people, I need your help.

When someone chooses a book, they often rely on reviews. A few kind words from you could:

- help someone take their first step toward healing.

- encourage another person to rebuild their resilience.

- inspire someone to reconnect with their body and inner peace.

- bring more light into someone's life.

It costs nothing, takes just a moment, but could change everything for someone searching for hope.

How to leave a review:

Simply scan the QR code below or visit the link below to share your thoughts.

https://www.amazon.com

If this book has helped you in any way, I'd love to hear about it—and so would others.

Thank you for being a part of this journey. Your generosity means the world to me.

Warmly,
Grace Bailey

Chapter 6

BEYOND THE BASICS:
ADVANCED TECHNIQUES

Using light to heal the body is one of the most noninvasive yet effective treatments we have.

–DR. JOSH AXE

Combining Therapies: Synergistic Effects With Other Treatments

INTRODUCING RED LIGHT THERAPY to your existing treatment plan opens the door to new possibilities in healing. When used alongside other therapies, it enhances the overall effect. Take physical therapy as an example. While it works to rebuild muscle and restore function, red light therapy can help reduce inflammation and speed up the repair process. Working synergistically together makes recovery quicker, smoother, and more comfortable.

Building on the concept of synergy, therapeutic combinations can be tailored to address targeted health concerns. For instance, in dermatology, combining red light therapy with topical antioxidant treatments can enhance results. Antioxidants are known to combat oxidative stress. When paired with red light therapy, they improve skin texture and accelerate the healing of blemishes and minor scars. This dual approach enriches the skin's resilience and vitality, offering an integrated solution for a radiant complexion.

Moreover, consider the potential in treating conditions like psoriasis. Red light therapy combined with emerging phototherapy techniques can precisely target afflicted skin areas while nourishing the surrounding tissues. This integrated treatment plan can be adapted based on individual responses, which involves fine-tuning the therapy's intensity and duration according to specific needs. The result is a personalized regimen that alleviates symptoms and fortifies the skin's structural integrity.

Expanding its therapeutic reach, red light therapy can complement medications used for managing chronic conditions. While pharmaceuticals target symptoms, red light therapy works at the cellular level to reduce inflammation and enhance function. Over time, this may lead to lower medication dosages and fewer side effects. For instance, an arthritis patient may find that regular light sessions increase the effectiveness of their treatment, easing pain and improving joint mobility. This integrated approach supports better outcomes and encourages a more holistic path to healing.

Red light therapy's potential is not limited to medical settings—it can also be effectively combined with holistic wellness practices. In a peaceful breathwork class, the warm glow of red light can align beautifully with the session's meditative atmosphere. This combination enhances relaxation, supports healing, and encourages a more immersive mind-body connection. Together, they foster a space where stress is gently released and overall well-being is improved.

Similarly, consider blending red light therapy with acupuncture. Acupuncture seeks to balance energy flow by targeting specific points in the body, an effect that red light therapy can elevate. The light penetrates the tissues, promoting healing at a cellular level, while acupuncture targets the body's energy pathways. Together, they form a synergy that maximizes the benefits of both practices.

Real-Life Success Stories and Integration Challenges

Real-life stories underscore the potential of these combinations. Take the case of post-operative patients incorporating red light therapy into their recovery process. By coupling it with prescribed rehabilitation exercises, they often experience reduced swelling and accelerated healing times, and improved strength and mobility.

Similarly, individuals managing chronic pain with red light therapy alongside mindfulness practices might find enhanced relief, as the calming effects of meditation synergize with the physical benefits of light exposure. For instance, patients suffering from chronic back pain have reported a marked improvement by integrating meditation with red light therapy. This blend reduces pain and fosters an environment for mental relaxation, which can be instrumental in pain management.

Managing a chronic condition like fibromyalgia often requires a combination of tools. When red light therapy is used alongside medication and lifestyle changes, many people experience lasting relief. The therapy helps reduce inflammation and supports cellular repair, offering a more complete approach to both physical and emotional health.

Despite its benefits, combining therapies presents its own set of challenges and considerations. Ensuring compatibility with existing treatments and consulting healthcare professionals before introducing new therapies are crucial for avoiding adverse interactions. These experts can craft a personalized plan that aligns with individual health needs, ensuring safety and efficacy. An example would be a diabetic patient exploring red light therapy for neuropathy; they need a customized approach to harmonize with their ongoing treatments. In fact, my chiropractor confirmed that he uses red light therapy for all his neuropathy patients.

Monitoring potential adverse interactions is equally important. Although red light therapy is generally safe, understanding how it interacts with medications or other treatments can avert complications. Regular consultations with healthcare providers inform and empower you to make necessary adjustments.

Visual Element: Integration Checklist—Appendix #1

The integration checklist found in Appendix #1 can be a valuable tool when combining therapies, offering a structured approach to ensure safety and effectiveness. It may include the following:

1. Consult with healthcare professionals

2. Schedule sessions appropriately

3. Monitor physical responses.

This checklist provides you with clear steps to navigate the complexities of integrative care. It can also include space to log baseline health metrics, track improvements, and record any side effects, which offers essential data for refining and personalizing your wellness plan.

Exploring these advanced techniques opens up possibilities for enhancing your wellness journey. By thoughtfully combining red light therapy with other treatments, you create a customized approach that supports your unique health goals. This integrative method amplifies therapeutic effects and fosters a deeper connection between mind and body, echoing the ancient wisdom of holistic healing with the precision of contemporary science.

DIY Innovations: Crafting Your Own Red Light Solutions—Appendix #2

For the DIY'ers, designing your own red light therapy device can be fulfilling and cost-effective, allowing you to tailor it precisely to your needs. A great starting point is building a custom LED array. This requires a few basic components: wavelength-specific LED bulbs, a power source, and a frame to hold it together. You can create a reliable and personalized light panel by soldering the LEDs onto a circuit board. For skin-level treatments, use LEDs in the 630–660 nanometer range, while deeper therapeutic goals require near-infrared LEDs in the 800–850 nanometer range. This DIY project offers a hands-on way to create a wellness tool built just for you.

You can expand on the idea by creating a portable red light therapy panel that adds a new level of convenience. A lightweight, battery-powered design lets you move the device around your home or bring it along with you while traveling. To build a more durable and mobile unit, you can also use materials like lightweight aluminum for the frame and incorporate rechargeable batteries. This portability ensures your therapy routine stays consistent, no matter where life takes you.

When evaluating DIY solutions against commercial devices, several considerations emerge. Cost-effectiveness stands out as a primary advantage of the DIY approach. Purchasing individual components typically costs less than acquiring a premade device, making it appealing for budget-conscious individuals. However, there are trade-offs. The durability of DIY devices may not match that of their commercial counterparts, which often undergo rigorous testing for sustained use. Therefore, DIY versions might require more frequent maintenance or adjustments.

Another critical factor to consider is safety. Commercial devices come with established safety standards and certifications, which provides a certain level of reassurance. In contrast, DIY projects necessitate meticulous attention to safety. Ensuring proper electrical measures are taken is imperative; for example, you must use insulated wires and confirm secure connections to prevent accidents. Additionally, verifying the accuracy of wavelengths ensures the desired therapeutic effects are achieved. Tools such as spectrometers can measure output, ensuring your homemade device operates as intended.

Customizing your therapy sessions opens the door to endless creativity. You might set your device to cycle through different light settings—one for relaxation in the evening, another for energizing your mornings. Adding aromatherapy enhances the experience even further. Diffusing essential oils like lavender or eucalyptus creates a calming atmosphere that complements the therapeutic effects of red light therapy. This thoughtful combination of light and scent turns each session into a restorative ritual for both body and mind.

Safety and efficacy remain non-negotiable aspects of any DIY project. Proper electrical safety measures protect both you and your device. Critical steps include double-checking connections before powering on and using insulated tools when handling electrical components. Regular wear-and-tear inspections and prompt replacement of damaged parts maintain functionality and safety.

Accuracy in wavelength is also vital for effectiveness. If your device emits the wrong wavelength, desired results may not materialize. Tools like spectrometers can verify output accuracy, ensuring your device meets therapeutic standards. Maintaining documentation of device specifications aids in troubleshooting, guides future enhancements, and ensures a consistent quality of therapy at home.

Creating DIY red light therapy solutions encourages you to merge creativity with practicality. With patience and attention to detail, you craft tools that cater specifically to your wellness goals. This approach deepens your understanding of red light therapy and enhances its integration into everyday life, transforming your home into a haven of personalized therapeutic care where innovation meets intention.

Biohacking With Light: Cutting-Edge Techniques

Biohacking is the practice of intentionally optimizing your body and mind through science-backed methods and self-experimentation. It allows you to take charge of your biology to perform, feel, and live better. Red light therapy is a powerful tool in this space. Beyond relaxation, it supports cognitive enhancement and recovery by stimulating blood flow and increasing oxygen to the brain. This gentle light transforms therapy into a strategic part of a lifestyle focused on clarity, vitality, and high performance.

The physical benefits are equally compelling. Athletes have long sought ways to expedite recovery, and targeted exposure to red light offers a viable solution. It accelerates muscle repair by reducing inflammation and promoting cellular regeneration. After a strenuous workout, a session can soothe tired muscles, diminishing downtime and enhancing performance. It's remarkable how simple exposure can make such a significant impact, converting fatigue into energy for subsequent workouts. Moreover, the application of red light therapy has found its niche in pre-competition preparations, where athletes use it strategically to enhance muscle endurance and resistance to muscle fatigue, thereby optimizing performance.

Advanced biohacking protocols offer techniques for optimizing specific outcomes. Let's discuss sleep, a precious commodity in today's fast-paced world. Using red light therapy before bed can revolutionize your nighttime routine. Exposing yourself to red light in the evening stimulates melatonin production, which regulates your sleep cycle and offers a natural way to calm the mind. It prepares the body for rest, enhancing sleep quality rather than accelerating sleep onset. Biohackers have reported experiencing better sleep, increased cognitive functions, and more balanced energy levels throughout the day as their bodies utilize rest more efficiently.

Hormonal balance is another benefit of red light therapy. Hormones influence everything from mood to metabolism, and achieving balance is vital for overall health. Specific light wavelengths can support hormonal equilibrium by enhancing glandular function. Routine sessions may stabilize mood swings and boost energy levels. It's about finding the sweet spot where your body synchronizes with its natural rhythm.

Biohackers are eager to share their experiences. One biohacker shared how integrating light therapy into his morning routine improved his productivity and outlook on life. Another emphasized the importance of consistency, noting that regular sessions led to noticeable physical and mental well-being improvements.

Expert advice underscores the need for safe practices in light biohacking. While it's easy to be swept away by the potential benefits, safety should remain paramount. Ensuring devices emit the appropriate wavelengths and using them as directed prevents overexposure and maximizes effectiveness. Experts advise starting with short sessions and gradually increasing exposure as your body adapts.

Looking ahead, the field of light biohacking presents promising possibilities. Emerging research suggests that specific wavelengths of light may one day be used to modulate gene expression—activating or suppressing specific genes to influence health outcomes. This innovative approach is drawing increasing interest as scientists explore how light interacts with our genetic code. Such advancements could pave the way for highly personalized healthcare strategies tailored to individual genetic profiles.

AI-driven biohacking programs that monitor wearable red light therapy (RLT) devices are emerging at the intersection of personalized wellness and smart technology. While fully integrated RLT wearables with AI capabilities are still developing, several platforms and devices are leading the way in combining photobiomodulation with intelligent health tracking:

Leading AI-Integrated RLT Wearables

- **Lumaflex Body Pro**

This wearable red light therapy device offers flexibility and portability, making it ideal for active individuals. It features app-based control, allowing users to customize sessions based on their activity levels and recovery needs. While not explicitly AI-driven, its smart features lay the groundwork for future AI integration.

- **FlexBeam by Recharge Health**

FlexBeam is a portable, targeted red light therapy device that adapts to various body areas. Its user-friendly interface and customizable treatment modes enable personalized therapy sessions. Though it doesn't currently employ AI, its design supports potential integration with AI-driven health platforms.

The intersection of technology and biology in biohacking presents a frontier rich with potential. As we explore these cutting-edge techniques, balancing innovation and caution remains crucial so we can ensure safe and effective practices that enhance our lives in tangible ways. By proactively engaging with these methods, individuals can exert greater control over their health destinies, exploring the limits of what their bodies can achieve.

Exploring Infrared: Expanding Your Light Spectrum

When we embrace the potential of infrared light, a world of deeper possibilities unfolds. Unlike red light, which primarily addresses skin-level concerns, infrared light dives beneath the surface. It penetrates deeper tissues, reaching muscles, joints, and even bones. This capability makes it a therapeutic powerhouse, offering benefits that red light alone cannot achieve. The thermal effects of infrared exposure further enhance its applications. Infrared light gently warms tissues, promoting increased blood flow and boosting the delivery of oxygen and nutrients to cells. This warmth can relax muscles and alleviate tension, making it a preferred choice for relieving tightness or discomfort.

Infrared light's therapeutic uses extend beyond red light therapy, offering diverse health benefits. Detoxification through infrared saunas is one such application. These saunas generate gentle heat and encourage sweating, which helps release toxins from the body. This process purifies and rejuvenates the body. Regular sessions in an infrared sauna can improve skin health, enhance circulation, and improve overall well-being. Users often describe heightened relaxation and clarity post-session, indicative of infrared's influence on physical and mental states.

For pain relief and muscle relaxation, infrared light is a game-changer. Its deep penetration allows it to target sore muscles and inflamed joints. For individuals experiencing chronic pain, such as arthritis or fibromyalgia, infrared therapy offers a soothing remedy. It alleviates discomfort by reducing inflammation and promoting healing at a cellular level. Athletes, too, benefit from infrared light for recovery. Following intense training, infrared therapy can accelerate muscle repair and reduce downtime, allowing athletes to maintain peak performance levels. These benefits also extend to non-athletes, supporting everyday mobility and quality of life.

Choosing and using infrared devices effectively requires an understanding of their nuances. When selecting a device, consider whether near or far-infrared light aligns with your goals. Near-infrared, which penetrates deeper, is often preferred for pain relief and muscle therapy. Conversely, far-infrared, with its pronounced thermal effects, is ideal for detoxification and relaxation. Balancing these options with your specific goals ensures you select the appropriate tool.

Optimal session lengths and frequencies vary based on individual needs. For most, sessions lasting 20–30 minutes several times a week provide significant benefits without the risk of overexposure. Finding a rhythm that integrates seamlessly into your lifestyle guarantees consistent benefits. Pay attention to your body's responses and adjust as necessary to enhance therapeutic outcomes.

Firsthand accounts offer a compelling look into the benefits of infrared light therapy. Athletes frequently recount how incorporating regular infrared sessions helped speed their recovery, reduce muscle soreness, and prepare them for their next challenge with greater ease. These experiences reflect the therapy's strong role in supporting physical performance.

Those living with chronic pain also find hope in infrared therapy. Someone with ongoing joint pain may describe how the deep, soothing warmth helped relieve discomfort and restore movement. These real-life stories remind us of the power of red light therapy to improve daily life for those managing long-term conditions.

As we explore these advanced techniques, it's evident that expanding your light spectrum with infrared creates new opportunities for health and wellness. The vast benefits offer solutions for both acute needs and long-term objectives. Whether your interest lies in detoxification, pain relief, or improved recovery, infrared therapy presents a meaningful opportunity to enrich self-care practices.

Benefits of Red Light Therapy for Animals

Red light therapy, is gaining popularity in veterinary medicine as a safe, noninvasive method to support healing and reduce pain in animals. Much like in humans, red and near-infrared light penetrate the skin and stimulate cellular energy production, helping to reduce inflammation, improve circulation, and promote tissue regeneration. Its wide-ranging applications make it a valuable tool for both acute injuries and chronic conditions in a variety of species.

In companion animals such as dogs and cats, red light therapy is commonly used to treat arthritis, joint pain, hip dysplasia, post-surgical wounds, and inflammatory skin conditions. It can also be highly beneficial in managing dental inflammation and promoting faster recovery from surgical procedures. For equine therapy, red light is often applied to sore backs, tendon injuries, and hoof conditions, helping horses recover more quickly from the demands of training and competition. Even smaller animals—rabbits, guinea pigs, and birds—can benefit from light therapy for wounds, infections, and mobility issues when administered carefully under professional guidance.

The treatment process typically involves using LED panels, handheld devices, or laser systems that emit specific wavelengths, usually in the range of 620–660 nanometers for red light and 810–850 nanometers for near-infrared. Red light targets surface-level issues like skin repair, while near-infrared penetrates deeper into muscle and joint tissue. Sessions may last anywhere from 5–20 minutes and are usually repeated several times per week during the initial phase of treatment. For more complex or chronic issues, continued maintenance sessions may be recommended.

Because it is drug-free, pain-free, and well-tolerated, red light therapy presents a gentle yet effective way to enhance an animal's quality of life. That said, it should always be used with appropriate caution—for example, avoiding application over cancerous growths or areas of active bleeding and protecting the animal's eyes if using a laser-based system. For best results, red light therapy should be used under the supervision of a licensed veterinarian, particularly when treating serious or complex conditions. As research continues to evolve, red light therapy is proving to be a valuable addition to holistic animal care given its potential to support recovery and wellness in a truly compassionate way.

In concluding this chapter, remember that exploring the multifaceted world of light therapy equips you with valuable tools for optimizing well-being. Each type of light offers distinct advantages, enabling you to tailor your approach to specific health goals. As we transition into the next chapter, consider how you might integrate these insights into a broader wellness plan that fortifies your holistic health journey with renewed vigor and understanding.

Chapter 7

ENHANCING YOUR
WELLNESS JOURNEY

RED LIGHT ISN'T JUST for your skin. It lifts your mood, clears your mind, and calms your nights.

–UNKNOWN

Nutrition and Red Light: Fueling Your Body for Optimal Results

Your body functions like a finely tuned instrument, with each nutrient playing a crucial role in your well-being. Just as a musician depends on the right composition, your system performs at its best when nourished with the right nutrients, especially those that work harmoniously with red light therapy. This nutritional alignment goes beyond general healthy eating; it involves a deeper understanding of how specific foods can amplify the benefits of your therapy sessions.

The foundation of this nutritional approach is the extraordinary impact of antioxidants. Naturally present in colorful fruits and vegetables, these compounds shield cells from oxidative damage and fuel their repair systems. With every antioxidant-rich meal, you strengthen your internal defense, enabling your cells to harness the full benefits of red light therapy. This simple dietary addition can elevate your healing potential from within.

The integration of nutrition and red light therapy creates a synergistic approach to health, with each element enhancing the effectiveness of the other. Omega-3 fatty acids, known for their powerful anti-inflammatory effects, are vital to this strategy. Salmon and plant-based options such as flaxseeds and walnuts are excellent sources of omega-3 fatty acids. These healthy fats support the body's natural healing processes. When combined with red light therapy, they help reduce inflammation, accelerate recovery, and promote overall well-being. This interaction highlights how nutrition and therapy can work hand in hand to support optimal health.

Vitamin D also stands out for its ability to support cellular health during therapy. Often referred to as the "sunshine vitamin," it plays a vital role in your body's light absorption capabilities, regulating calcium and phosphate levels essential for healthy bones and muscles. This function complements red light therapy's myriad benefits while enhancing bodily performance. Magnesium, often overlooked, is crucial for energy production at the cellular level. It is a cofactor in over 300 enzymatic processes, including those pivotal in adenosine triphosphate (ATP) production—the very energy currency red light therapy aims to enhance.

One of the best ways to amplify the effects of red light therapy is by fueling your body with nutrient-rich whole foods. Meals centered around fresh greens, colorful vegetables, and plant-based staples like grains, legumes, and nuts deliver the nourishment your cells need to thrive. This anti-inflammatory approach helps create a balanced internal environment, allowing nutrition and therapy to work together to support your energy, recovery, and overall vitality.

The Power of Superfoods

Beyond the conventional array of fruits and vegetables, certain superfoods are instrumental in elevating your nutritional regimen to a new level. Chia seeds, renowned for their high omega-3 content and abundant fiber, support digestion and inflammation control. Chia seeds absorb liquid and expand more than 10 times their original size, which is a perfect representation of their capacity to aid digestion and reduce inflammation within the body.

Spirulina, a nutrient-dense, blue-green algae, delivers a substantial supply of protein, essential vitamins, and powerful antioxidants. Beyond basic nutrition, superfoods like this contain bioactive compounds that may complement and enhance the therapeutic effects of red light therapy. Incorporating them into your routine supports a more integrated and effective approach to overall wellness.

Probiotics are key microorganisms for your wellness. Found in fermented foods such as kimchi, sauerkraut, and yogurt, they help maintain a balanced gut microbiome, which is an essential part of immune health and nutrient absorption. A healthy digestive system supports your body's ability to respond to therapies like red light therapy, helping you achieve more impactful and sustained results.

When aligned with red light therapy, meal planning evolves into a mindful practice that enhances healing from within. The nutrients you consume—especially when timed thoughtfully—can shape your body's response. A vibrant, antioxidant-rich breakfast like a berry and spinach smoothie with chia seeds energizes your cells and creates a foundation for a more powerful therapeutic experience.

Recovery meals following therapy are essential for giving your body the tools it needs to heal and thrive. A nourishing dish—such as quinoa with grilled chicken, avocado, and pumpkin seeds—offers a powerful mix of protein for muscle repair, beneficial fats for brain support, and magnesium to restore energy. Each bite helps reinforce the benefits of your therapy session and supports your wellness from the inside out.

> **Interactive Element: Meal Planning Exercise**
> Creating meal plans that supplement therapy days can be both enjoyable and rewarding. One approach is to create weekly menus that include pre-therapy breakfasts and post-therapy dinners. Experiment with recipes incorporating antioxidant-rich ingredients and omega-3s, tailoring them to suit personal preferences or dietary restrictions. A sample weekly menu is provided in Appendix #3.

These dietary adjustments epitomize a holistic approach to wellness that complements the multifaceted benefits of red light therapy. Integrating these nutritionally dense foods into your routine fuels your body and unlocks your potential to live a vibrant, healthy lifestyle.

Think about the impact these small, intentional changes could have on your overall wellness. Embracing the powerful connection between what you eat and how your body heals may open doors to deeper vitality and lasting health. With every nutrient-rich meal, you amplify the benefits of red light therapy, making each session more effective and meaningful.

Exercise and Light: Maximizing Your Workouts

Entering your workout space with more energy and focus can give you the edge needed to break through plateaus. Red light therapy helps make this possible by improving stamina and resilience through enhanced mitochondrial activity. When your cells generate energy more efficiently, you can push through intense training, finish strong, and unlock new performance levels, such as lifting heavier, running faster.

Recovery is just as vital as the workout itself, and this is where red light therapy proves exceptionally beneficial. It helps reduce muscle soreness and supports faster recovery by minimizing inflammation and encouraging cellular repair. Regular use can significantly shorten downtime after intense exercise, allowing for a quicker return to training. For those serious about fitness progression, this therapy becomes a powerful tool in sustaining performance and preventing burnout.

Strategically fitting therapy into your fitness regimen allows you to reap its benefits, but it requires attention to timing. Start with pre-exercise activation sessions. For example, a 10-minute session prior to hitting the gym effectively "wakes up" your muscles and prepares them for the workout. It's similar to stretching but targeted at your cellular infrastructure. Post-exercise recovery optimization is also key. A short session aids in soothing muscles, alleviating stiffness, and ensuring readiness for the next challenge thrown your way.

Real-World Success Stories and Best Practices

Real-life applications continue to highlight the powerful synergy between red light therapy and fitness routines. Marathon runners, known for enduring immense physical strain, frequently face extended recovery periods. However, those incorporating red light therapy report noticeably faster recovery, allowing for more consistent training and improved performance. Weightlifters also benefit from accelerated muscle repair and strength gains, enabling them to progress with reduced post-workout soreness.

Selecting the right workout to complement red light therapy can significantly enhance its impact. High-intensity internal training (HIIT), praised for its time efficiency and cardiovascular benefits, aligns well with the therapy's ability to boost endurance and speed recovery. The alternating bursts of effort and rest in HIIT are supported by the therapy's role in energy optimization and inflammation reduction, helping athletes recover swiftly and train harder.

In addition, yoga and flexibility routines form a natural pairing with red light therapy. The therapy supports joint health and mobility, allowing smoother transitions and more fluid movement during practice. Its soothing effect also deepens yoga's meditative qualities, offering a balanced physical and mental wellness approach.

A structured weekly chart that blends red light therapy with various exercise modalities can be a helpful tool to support implementation. This visual guide can help you maintain consistency, monitor progress, and focus on well-rounded fitness and recovery habits. Refer to the sample workout schedule provided in Appendix #4.

Furthermore, diversifying your workout strategies by incorporating resistance training and aerobic exercises can further establish a holistic approach. Weight training strengthens muscles, while red light therapy can assist in rapid recovery. Meanwhile, cardiovascular exercises like cycling or swimming complement therapy by promoting heart health and improving stamina. These combined efforts work harmoniously to cover all facets of fitness, providing a balanced and comprehensive wellness system.

The goal isn't simply to push harder or lift more—it's to train smarter. When red light therapy complements your fitness routine, you're enhancing your mental resilience and physical fortitude without compromising recovery or risking burnout.

Red light therapy has immense potential to integrate seamlessly into your lifestyle and specific fitness aspirations. Whether you're an athlete striving for personal bests or an enthusiast aiming to sustain general health and vitality, this therapy integration holds the potential key to unlocking unparalleled performance targets with assurance and resilience.

Stress Management: Light as a Tool for Relaxation

In our fast-paced world, stress is all too common. Fortunately, red light therapy offers an innovative pathway toward relaxation by gently steering your body's stress responses into calmer states. The therapy excels in lowering cortisol levels—the hormone often referred to as the "stress hormone"—which, when elevated, inflicts havoc on both body and mind. By diminishing cortisol, you may notice a heightened sense of ease, feeling less frazzled by the pressures of daily life. This isn't just about feeling good; it's about empowering your body to engage its parasympathetic nervous system, which is responsible for rest and digestion. When this system is regulated, your heart rate slows, your muscles relax, and your mind finds a quieter space to rejuvenate.

Red light therapy can be a powerful addition to mindfulness and relaxation techniques. When integrated into meditation, the therapy's soft illumination helps foster mental clarity and heightened awareness. Its warmth enhances sensory engagement, deepening your connection to the moment. Similarly, pairing red light therapy with structured breathing exercises can amplify their calming effect. Each breath becomes more intentional, promoting a fuller sense of relaxation and emotional balance.

Stories of Relaxation and Renewal

Real-life experiences bring the power of red light therapy into focus. Jess, a high-performing professional navigating constant pressure, found moments of calm during her midday breaks by pairing red light therapy with guided breathing. These short sessions helped her reset so she could return to work with sharper focus and renewed energy. Tom, a dedicated caregiver often consumed by the needs of others, introduced evening sessions into his routine. This calming ritual provided a much-needed pause, easing his transition into restful sleep. Together, their stories highlight how integrating therapy into daily routines can create lasting relief from stress.

Incorporating complementary practices can significantly elevate the stress-relief benefits of red light therapy. Mindfulness, which emphasizes present-moment awareness, helps reduce anxiety by redirecting focus away from past regrets or future concerns. When paired with therapy, it deepens the experience of calm and mental clarity. Another valuable technique is progressive muscle relaxation, which involves intentionally tensing and releasing muscle groups. When practiced under red light, this method helps dissolve physical tension and promotes a profound sense of relaxation.

In a serene environment, the warm tones of red light therapy cast a calming ambiance as you settle into stillness. With each deep breath, the body naturally relaxes, releasing stored tension and inviting calm. This simple yet powerful moment of focused presence can be a transformative addition to daily life, helping shift high-stress situations into moments of peace and clarity.

Consistent engagement with red light therapy nurtures an inner calmness that stands resilient to life's unexpected storms. While stress is an inevitable element of life, it needn't dictate your experience. The beauty of using therapy for stress management lies in its versatility and potential for integration with meditation and deep breathing practices.

Sleep Enhancement: Improving Rest With Red Light

Red light therapy has shown significant promise in improving sleep quality, particularly for individuals facing insomnia or disrupted rest. By stimulating the production of melatonin, the hormone responsible for regulating sleep-wake cycles, this therapy helps guide the body into a state of readiness for sleep. Beyond simply helping you fall asleep faster, it promotes more restorative and uninterrupted rest.

Furthermore, red light therapy plays an important role in supporting your circadian rhythm, the body's internal clock that regulates sleep and wake cycles. When this rhythm is aligned, you wake feeling refreshed and ready for the day. Incorporating evening sessions into your routine can create a peaceful transition into rest. Use this time as a personal sanctuary, a moment to disconnect and prepare for deep, restorative sleep. The soft glow of red light gently cues your body to relax, easing you into a state of calm.

Consistency is vital here. Regular therapy sessions assist in conditioning your body's natural rhythms, steadily leading to enhanced sleep quality. Allocating evening time for therapy helps you create a soothing ritual that prepares your body for rest. The meditative nature of red light therapy can make bedtime an anticipated moment of the day, enveloping you in a sensation of serenity and restoration.

Personal Transformations Through Better Sleep

Red light therapy's magic isn't just in the research—it's in the stories of people like Ella and Mark. Ella had battled insomnia for years, and most remedies barely made a dent. However, she noticed a difference when she started using red light therapy before bed: it became easier to fall asleep, and she woke up less through the night. Mark, a night-shift worker whose sleep routine was all over the place, experienced similar benefits. Red light therapy helped him reset his circadian rhythm and finally feel rested again. These experiences show how effective this therapy can be in supporting better, deeper sleep.

Sleep quality improves when red light therapy is paired with mindful bedtime practices. Good sleep hygiene—like setting a consistent schedule, creating a tranquil space, and limiting blue light exposure before bed—lays the groundwork for restorative rest. Complementing your routine with essential oils known for calming effects, such as lavender or chamomile, adds another layer of relaxation. Together, these practices create a nurturing bedtime ritual that encourages deeper, more restful sleep.

Incorporating additional calming elements—such as lavender aromatherapy and white noise—into your nightly red light therapy session can significantly enhance the body's transition into sleep. These tools help promote deep relaxation, supporting a smoother shift from wakefulness to rest. This multi-faceted strategy blends therapeutic light with sensory relaxation techniques, offering a well-rounded path to improved sleep quality and overall recovery.

The journey toward untroubled slumber through red light therapy is uniquely personal. It requires exploration to identify the most effective methods for you and the best ways integrate them into your nightly routine. Perhaps a warm bath prior to therapy makes you feel more relaxed, or journaling helps clear cluttered thoughts before bed. Together, these minor adjustments can drastically impact how well you sleep and how invigorated you feel in the morning.

To support and fine-tune your routine, try incorporating a weekly reflection exercise. Take a few minutes at the end of each week to document your post-therapy experiences and note any patterns in your sleep quality. This simple practice allows for effective tracking and helps you identify areas for adjustment and optimization.

What makes red light therapy truly special is how well it harmonizes with the rhythms of your life. It doesn't ask for disruption—it supports and enhances what's already working. When you welcome this therapy into your routine, you create space for deeper rest and brighter days, all while keeping things simple and sustainable.

Emotional Well-Being: Red Light's Impact on Mental Health

Red light therapy is gaining recognition as a supportive, noninvasive approach to mental wellness. It has been shown to naturally increase serotonin levels, a key neurotransmitter involved in mood regulation. By stimulating serotonin production, red light therapy can help promote emotional balance and improve resilience during difficult periods. For individuals managing symptoms of depression, it may offer a valuable complementary tool for emotional support.

Integrating red light therapy into a mental health regimen can yield considerable benefits. Many individuals find it particularly effective in addressing Seasonal affective disorder (SAD), the dip in mood typically experienced during darker months. Regular red light exposure mimics sunlight's effects, alleviating symptoms, delivering a positive mood uplift, and contributing to long-term mood stabilization.

Healing Through Personal Experiences

Personal experiences illustrate the profound effects red light therapy can have on emotional well-being. Amy, who lived with chronic anxiety, found significant relief after incorporating the therapy into her routine. Over time, she experienced a level of calm that had long eluded her, allowing her to engage more fully in daily life. Jake, a mental health advocate, shared that consistent sessions helped ease his depressive symptoms, contributing to increased clarity and emotional balance. These testimonials highlight the potential of red light therapy to support mental health care.

For even greater support, it helps to blend therapy sessions with other mental wellness tools. Journaling is a powerful way to process emotions and track progress; for example, writing down thoughts after a session can reveal insights you might otherwise miss. Over time, this self-awareness builds a stronger foundation for growth. Creative expression, such as painting or sketching, is another wonderful addition, offering a soothing outlet that pairs beautifully with the calming effects of red light therapy.

Creative activities take on new depth when paired with the warm presence of red light therapy. Sitting quietly with a journal or sketchbook after a session allows thoughts to unfold naturally, supported by the calm energy surrounding you. These moments often become more than just creative outlets—they evolve into tools for reflection and emotional release. Over time, these practices help build resilience and provide space for clarity, healing, and insight.

As we wrap up this chapter, consider how red light therapy can gently find its place within your mental health routine, offering support in subtle and significant ways. This chapter explored its potential to support your emotional well-being through biological processes and lifestyle integration. But remember: Your experience is uniquely your own, and finding what works may take experimentation and time. Exploration is part of the growth process.

Next, we'll read real life stories of the transformative power of red light therapy across diverse lifestyles and activities. As we continue, remain curious—you're building a toolkit tailored to your needs.

Chapter 8

PERSONAL STORIES AND TESTIMONIALS

Let your body remember how to shine—cell by cell, breath by breath, light by light.

–UNKNOWN

Transformative Journeys: Personal Success Stories

ROSEMARY, A NEW MOTHER navigating the challenges of early parenthood, found herself physically depleted and emotionally drained. The demands of caring for her infant left little space for self-care or renewal. Then, she noticed a remarkable transformation after introducing red light therapy into her routine. Increased energy and mental clarity allowed her to re-engage with daily life and reconnect with her identity beyond motherhood. "I never imagined light could make such a difference," she reflected, noting her new feelings of empowerment and balance.

Rosemary's narrative exemplifies the broader sense of renewal that comes with striking a balance between caring for others and oneself. Previously, she felt constrained by the demands of her household, leaving scant time for personal rejuvenation. But with red light therapy, she could carve out essential moments for self-care, transforming her experience of motherhood from sheer survival to one of joy and growth.

George, a retiree, once believed his most active years were behind him. His days had fallen into a predictable rhythm, lacking energy and excitement. That changed with the introduction of red light therapy. What began as a simple wellness practice soon sparked a dramatic shift. He began waking up with renewed energy, purpose, and passion that he used to immerse himself in local projects and volunteering. "This therapy has been a revelation," he said.

His journey reminds us that meaningful engagement has no age limit. Energized by daily sessions, George reconnected with his community, mentoring young adults and participating in neighborhood initiatives. Each morning became an opportunity for contribution and connection, proving that post-retirement life can be as vibrant as any chapter before it.

Red light therapy has made a difference in many lives, from high-performing executives to imaginative creators. Stress had become a constant companion for Emily, an executive navigating the daily storm of deadlines and decisions. Red light therapy offered her the calm she desperately needed. With each session, she felt her mind clear and her stress ease. "Amid the chaos, I found my center," she admitted.

The relief she found wasn't just personal—it became a catalyst for change. Realizing how profoundly the therapy had helped her, Emily took the lead in introducing wellness practices into her workplace. Her advocacy sparked a shift toward a healthier, more balanced company culture.

Creative individuals like Jake have also harnessed the benefits of red light therapy to enhance their artistic practice. Faced with recurring creative blocks and mental fatigue, Jake sought a solution that would restore his focus. He experienced improved mental clarity through regular therapy sessions, allowing ideas to emerge more naturally and with greater depth. This revitalization led to a series of artworks that captured his distinct creative voice.

Jake's experience illustrates the powerful connection between cognitive wellness and creative expression. As his mental fog lifted, he could innovate freely, exploring new artistic techniques and perspectives. Red light therapy became integral to his creative process, offering the clarity and energy needed to break through limitations and explore new frontiers in his work.

During some routine maintenance on my property, I witnessed red light therapy's impact firsthand. My contractor, Jerry, was struggling with significant shoulder pain and limited mobility, so I let him try my LightStim handheld pain-relief device. After just one 30-minute session, he reported substantial relief and was able to continue his work without discomfort.

These stories showcase resilience in spirit, no matter the individual's background. The common thread is an unwavering determination, which stems from a refusal to accept limitations and a burning desire to reclaim control over their lives. For many, red light therapy isn't merely a health hack but a powerful reminder of hope that can reignite passion and purpose.

Some people will struggle with overcoming initial self-doubt regarding the practicality of red light therapy. However, the individuals in our stories witnessed their skepticism transform into belief as results unfolded. Establishing a consistent routine was key, as each session reinforced their commitment to personal growth. Life, with its myriad of challenges, work demands, and family responsibilities may have tested their resolve, but they persevered, driven by the promise of transformation. "I never thought I'd find something so simple yet so impactful," one user noted. Another described the therapy as a "light at the end of a dark tunnel," offering hope where there was once despair.

> **Reflection Section**
> Pause and reflect: How might red light therapy fit into your life? Contemplate its potential impact on your personal journey, noting thoughts or experiences. Consider how you could create space for consistency, the foundational element of any successful therapeutic endeavor.

These testimonials transcend mere stories, affirming human resilience and adaptability. They remind us of the possibility of change, regardless of our starting point or the obstacles we face. Through shared experiences, we find solidarity—a reminder that we're not alone in our struggles or triumphs.

What makes red light therapy so compelling is its universal appeal and adaptability. It crosses age groups, professions, and life experiences, supporting everything from postnatal recovery to high-level career demands. No matter your journey, this therapy offers a way to reconnect with energy, balance, and a deeper sense of self.

As these personal accounts illustrate, its potential impact is far-reaching. Exploring how it aligns with your goals could mark the beginning of meaningful change. Sometimes, the first step is simply allowing yourself to engage with new possibilities.

Athlete Experiences: Red Light in Sports and Recovery

Competitive sports is a high-stakes career, and many athletes must constantly seek innovative methods to gain a performance edge. Red light therapy has gained recognition as a powerful tool, especially among elite performers. Olympic athletes, for example, have incorporated it into their rigorous training regimens to support recovery and optimize physical readiness. As a pre-competition ritual, the therapy offers a moment of calm focus, helping athletes ground themselves before stepping into the spotlight.

Weekend warriors who push their limits after a long week at the office are discovering new stamina levels with red light therapy. Its potential to accelerate recovery and reduce strain empowers them to keep going when others might slow down. For example, a sprinter might use it to bounce back between runs, staying sharp and competitive. Cyclists battling persistent knee pain often rely on its calming effects to ride longer, stronger, and with purpose.

Coaches and sports professionals have observed these transformations firsthand. Many extol red light therapy as a critical addition to athletic training, lauding its capacity to enhance recovery and minimize injury risks. Professional trainers vouch for its efficacy, noting its ability to diminish muscle soreness and fatigue. Sports physiotherapists recommend it to clients, emphasizing its benefits in managing pain and improving performance outcomes.

In a sport where every millisecond counts, swimmers seek every possible edge, and red light therapy has become part of that winning formula. It supports their training by loosening tight muscles and helping the body recover faster, which allows them to stay in top form. With less physical strain, swimmers can fine-tune their skills and build endurance. At the same time, the calming effect of therapy strengthens their mental focus and reinforces a deep sense of purpose—two key ingredients in rising to the challenge of elite competition.

Red light therapy's psychological benefits are as impactful as its physical advantages. In competitive sports, mental resilience often determines the outcome, making focus and emotional control essential attributes. Red light therapy gives athletes a competitive edge by enhancing mental clarity and reducing stress. Whether it's a tennis player maintaining calm during high-stakes serves or a swimmer staying centered amidst intense competition, this therapy helps preserve sharpness and composure under pressure.

These athletes find that red light therapy doesn't just heal their bodies; it sharpens their minds, creating an internal sanctuary where they can regroup, gather strength, and tackle challenges with revitalized vigor. For many, this therapy is essential to their mental preparation, fostering resilience and enhancing confidence.

However, what truly distinguishes this therapy is its broad accessibility. It isn't confined to elite athletes with access to high-end facilities. Weekend warriors, amateur athletes, and fitness enthusiasts alike reap its benefits, favoring its simple yet effective approach. Its versatility allows it to be used conveniently at home or on the go, smoothly integrating into any lifestyle.

Athletes from various disciplines share parallel tales of triumph with red light therapy. The overarching theme is progress—not solely in physical performance but in overall well-being. They discover a newfound balance between pushing limits and nurturing their bodies, recognizing that recovery is as vital as exertion.

For many athletes, red light therapy signifies more than an enhancement to their training regimen; it symbolizes hope and potential. Through their stories, we can also discover inspiration. Their journeys remind us that anything is achievable with determination, appropriate tools, and the support of red light therapy.

Chronic Pain Warriors: Overcoming Pain With Light

Chronic pain can be an overwhelming and persistent challenge, often leaving individuals feeling trapped by their condition. For many, red light therapy has emerged as a noninvasive, effective solution. Carla, diagnosed with fibromyalgia, faced daily pain that limited her mobility and joy in everyday activities. After committing to consistent therapy sessions, she experienced a noticeable reduction in symptoms. The improvement allowed her to reconnect with family life and resume activities she once loved, like gardening. Reflecting on her journey, she shared, "I feel like I can finally breathe again," highlighting the therapy's emotional and physical relief.

Next, consider Michael, a veteran confronting service-related injuries that left him in perpetual discomfort. The physical toll was massive, but it was the emotional scars that inflicted deeper wounds. Red light therapy helped him manage pain and rebuild his life. Each session improved his mobility, enabling him to reclaim activities he once thought lost forever. His transition from reliance on painkillers to a holistic approach incorporating therapy marked a pivotal change in his healing journey. "This isn't just about managing pain; it's about living life again," he said with newfound optimism.

Beyond the physical aspect of healing, Michael's journey underscores identity restoration. He was able to re-engage with activities he loved, finding a newfound purpose that was once overshadowed by pain. His journey resonated within his community, inspiring fellow veterans and raising awareness about alternative pain management practices.

The journey toward pain relief through red light therapy often leads to unexpected emotional healing. Those who have carried the weight of chronic discomfort for years frequently find themselves letting go of the fear and anxiety that once shaped their daily choices. When pain dominates, it's easy to withdraw and lose confidence. But as the therapy soothes the body, it also revives the spirit, creating space for joy, connection, and a renewed sense of belonging.

Individuals report feeling more present in social settings and less burdened by the looming shadow of discomfort. With pain no longer dictating their lives, they engage more fully with loved ones and partake in community activities, experiencing an emotional renaissance.

Healthcare providers have taken note of these benefits, too. Dr. Emily Hughes, a practitioner specializing in pain management, witnessed firsthand her patients' profound changes. "I've seen remarkable improvements in my patients," she observed. "Red Light Therapy has become an indispensable tool in our treatment arsenal." Therapists echo this sentiment, highlighting the therapy's capacity to support traditional methods without adverse effects. "It's not just about reducing pain; it's about enhancing quality of life," said one therapist who regularly integrates red light therapy into their practice.

This shift from medication dependency to a holistic strategy is a journey many chronic pain warriors undertake. It involves lifestyle adaptations, including regular therapy sessions, exercise, and mindfulness practices. The result is often a significant reduction in medication use, leading to fewer side effects and improved overall health.

These personal narratives underscore red light therapy's versatility and impact on chronic pain management. Each story is unique yet shares common themes: resilience, determination, and hope. Individuals once trapped in cycles of pain have found liberation and empowerment through regular therapy use. By addressing both the physical and emotional aspects of chronic pain, the therapy fosters a holistic healing approach that deeply resonates with those seeking relief.

Reflecting on these experiences, it's apparent that red light therapy provides more than a temporary reprieve; it offers a clear path to lasting change. For many chronic pain warriors, it signifies a new chapter—one characterized by possibility rather than limitation. Whether reclaiming hobbies, strengthening relationships, or waking up without the dread of persistent pain, red light therapy profoundly impacts countless lives.

Through these stories, we learn that overcoming chronic pain involves more than alleviating symptoms; it allows individuals to reclaim their life's joys and look forward to a future unburdened by past struggles. Red light therapy is a catalyst for transformation, enabling individuals to rewrite their narratives with light leading the way.

Skin Transformation: Real Results From Real People

Like many teens, Lily faced the emotional weight of acne, with each flare-up quietly chipping away at her self-confidence. Mirrors became reminders of what she wanted to hide rather than celebrate. When she began using red light therapy, progress was gradual but powerful. With each session, her skin became clearer, and her confidence grew stronger. Her journey wasn't just about clearer skin but about reclaiming pride and learning to embrace herself fully. Lily's story shows how personal struggles can transform into triumphs with the right support.

For adults like Mark, signs of aging often feel like unwelcome reminders of time passing. Fine lines and age spots seemingly appear overnight, each one marking years lived. Red light therapy offered Mark an opportunity to rewrite that narrative. The therapy didn't just smooth his skin; it rekindled a youthful glow that radiated with each smile. Mark found himself standing taller and feeling more hopeful, as if the therapy had peeled back layers of time to reveal who he once was and still could be. This newfound radiance did wonders for his self-image, allowing him to engage more fully and confidently with life.

The impact of visual documentation in tracking progress should not be overlooked. Before-and-after comparisons provide compelling evidence of red light therapy's effectiveness. A visual timeline of skin improvements captures the subtle yet meaningful changes that occur over time, showcasing reduced pigmentation and the gradual fading of scars. These visuals aren't mere images; they are stories of resilience and renewal that are etched in the skin and representative of red light therapy's potential.

Enhanced skin health frequently leads to improved self-perception. Confidence is crucial for professionals like Jane, who often found herself in the spotlight at public speaking engagements. Jane's struggle with skin issues made her hesitant to address an audience. However, as red light therapy worked its magic, her confidence soared. She was no longer preoccupied with hiding imperfections and could instead concentrate on delivering her message with clarity and poise. This newfound assurance transformed her professional life, opening doors to opportunities she had previously avoided.

Even the slightest change can spark a breakthrough in a field where every detail matters. Emma, a model struggling with self-doubt and professional setbacks, found renewed hope through red light therapy. As her skin improved, so did her confidence—enabling her to return to the spotlight with strength and poise. What followed was a revitalization of her career and a more confident belief in herself. Her story is a powerful reminder of how external changes can fuel internal growth and open doors to unexpected opportunities.

Dermatologists and skincare experts have taken notice of these transformations. Dr. Lin, a renowned dermatologist, remarked on the efficacy of red light therapy: "The results are both remarkable and scientifically supported." Such endorsements bolster the therapy's credibility in the skincare domain. Experts like Dr. Lin have successfully integrated red light therapy into their practices, witnessing firsthand its ability to deliver authentic results for patients seeking renewal and rejuvenation.

These stories paint a vivid picture of the physical and emotional transformation that red light therapy can inspire. It doesn't just erase blemishes or smooth wrinkles; it unveils the confidence that comes from feeling comfortable in one's own skin. Anyone, from a teenager facing adolescent trials or an adult wishing to defy time's marks, can discover empowerment, self-assurance, and renewed enthusiasm for life with red light therapy.

Community Voices: Diverse Testimonials

To illustrate the far-reaching benefits of red light therapy, let's explore a few more stories. First, there's Rosa, a vibrant 70-year-old living in a bustling city who rediscovered her energy through neighborhood walks, her arthritis pain lessening with each therapy session. Then there's Jamal, a young entrepreneur from a small town, juggling multiple startups while battling chronic fatigue. Red light therapy became his secret weapon; it revitalized his energy levels, enhanced his clarity, and enabled him to drive his ventures forward with renewed vigor.

In her small farming community, Maria, a mother of three, found a way to ease chronic joint pain without relying on regular doctor appointments. For her, the therapy became a form of self-care in a place where medical access is limited. Meanwhile, Tom, thriving in the high-pressure world of urban finance, discovered the therapy's power to reduce stress and sharpen focus, helping him stay grounded amid the hustle. These stories reflect how one therapy can meet very different needs in very different places.

These stories encapsulate red light therapy's universal appeal, including its ability to transcend socioeconomic boundaries. Whether residing in high-rise apartments or countryside cottages, the therapy's accessibility renders it invaluable for many. A teacher in a well-funded suburb might use it to sustain health amidst a demanding school year; at the same time, a factory worker might rely on it to alleviate back pain after long shifts. The commonality is clear: The therapy seamlessly integrates into diverse lifestyles and can bring about significant improvements.

At the heart of these narratives lies a shared theme of hope and transformation, beginning with skepticism and evolving into life-altering results. For instance, Ellen, initially doubtful of its efficacy for her migraines, found herself pleasantly surprised by the reduced frequency and intensity of her headaches. Her story resonates with countless others who transitioned from uncertainty to immense gratitude for the positive changes they've experienced.

Community feedback amplifies these voices, with online forums and support groups transforming into vibrant spaces where users share experiences and tips. People like Kevin, initially relying solely on medication for his depression, found solace in these communities. Encouraged by others' success stories with red light therapy, he opted to give it a try. His journey became one of shared learning and support, where he found comfort and practical advice from those treading similar paths. Red light therapy doesn't just offer individual gains—it supports collective growth, mutual encouragement, and a sense of community where people uplift each other with every shared success.

In closing this chapter, it's evident that red light therapy extends beyond just a health tool, emerging as a conduit that connects people through shared stories and experiences. These voices exemplify the therapy's extensive reach and profound life impact across various aspects. As we venture into the next chapter, we'll explore how to integrate these insights into practical, everyday wellness applications.

Chapter 9

EMBRACING A
TECH-FORWARD
APPROACH

Light up your performance. Red light therapy boosts energy production where it matters most—inside your muscles.

–UNKNOWN

The Future of Light Therapy: Innovations on the Horizon

AI IS REVOLUTIONIZING HEALTHCARE, and red light therapy is embracing its potential. Modern devices now go beyond basic functions by analyzing your skin's texture and moisture levels and delivering custom sessions based on that data. This smart technology offers a new level of accuracy, using detailed information to create practical care routines that adjust with your body's needs, all without leaving your home.

Research breakthroughs in how specific wavelengths affect the body are unlocking new potential for red light therapy. By honing in on precise frequencies, treatments can now focus more effectively on issues like inflammation and chronic pain. This level of accuracy allows for more personalized care, making it possible to address conditions such as autoimmune disorders or sports injuries with greater success. It represents a powerful shift toward more efficient, targeted, and holistic healing.

Red light therapy is poised to move beyond its current applications, with growing interest in its potential within emerging areas of health and wellness. One of the most compelling frontiers is neurotherapy, where RLT may support brain health, help manage neurological disorders, and enhance everyday cognitive performance.

This evolving science suggests potential benefits in mental health care as well, such as complementing existing treatments for anxiety and depression, particularly when paired with mindfulness practices. These developments are not speculative but grounded in ongoing research into the dynamic relationship between light exposure and human physiology. Similarly, dermatological advancements show promise. Red light therapy may offer effective, noninvasive solutions for chronic skin conditions like psoriasis and eczema, delivering long-term relief where conventional treatments fall short.

With each advancement in health tech, red light therapy is becoming even more adaptive and personalized. Wearable health monitors now have the potential to sync directly with red light therapy devices, creating a responsive therapy experience that adjusts in real time. By tapping into biometric feedback—like heart rate variability, skin temperature, or inflammation markers—your device can fine-tune each session for maximum impact. This intelligent interaction also enables live monitoring of healing progress, bringing therapy into a smarter, data-driven future.

Virtual reality (VR) is opening new doors for wellness by working alongside red light therapy to create more engaging and relaxing treatment experiences. By combining soothing VR environments with the physical benefits of RLT, recovery can become faster and more comfortable. This blend of technology helps make therapy feel more complete, supporting mental calm while the body heals. With VR, users are placed in peaceful settings that promote focus and enhance the overall effectiveness of each session.

While these innovations point to exciting progress, they also raise important concerns, especially regarding regulation and ethics. Technology often moves faster than policies can keep up, making it crucial to build systems that protect users while allowing innovation to thrive. Privacy is another key issue, as AI and wearable devices collect sensitive personal data. To ensure responsible growth, experts stress the need for strong ethical standards that guide the development and use of these technologies.

Challenges aside, the future of red light therapy is unfolding in exciting ways. With new tech pushing boundaries, it's quickly becoming a cornerstone of personalized health care. Whether you're exploring it for the first time or are already a fan, this is a great moment to experience the shift that's redefining how we think about healing and well-being.

Progress in wellness hinges on welcoming innovation built on proven scientific foundations. Being informed not only deepens understanding but also unlocks the true potential of emerging technologies. As these tools naturally integrate into our everyday routines, they spark a wider transformation, elevating personal wellness into a state of connected, empowered living.

The rapid pace of health tech invites you to take an active role in shaping your wellness journey. Whether you're using smart devices or exploring next-gen therapies, you're not just along for the ride—you're helping lead the way. By embracing red light therapy through a tech-forward lens, you're aligning with innovation that empowers personal health breakthroughs like never before.

Apps and Gadgets for Therapy Tracking

The synergy between wellness and innovation is clearly reflected in how red light therapy is managed through smart technology. Today's mobile apps function as personalized wellness guides, enriching sessions with more than just scheduling. Features like adaptive timing, goal tracking, and animated progress insights bring a new level of precision and engagement to your health journey. If you're someone who loves exploring the latest in wearable tech, this is exciting progress. Just keep in mind that the apps available right now are still limited, since the technology is still in its early days.

The merging of technology with wellness fosters a more active, engaged relationship with red light therapy. Smart apps do more than track progress—they create structure, consistency, and motivation. When data is presented as visual milestones—like energy gains or visible skin improvements—it transforms the experience, making progress feel personal and achievable. Built-in feedback loops and milestone recognition encourage adherence, reinforcing each small success.

As wearable devices evolve, they become central to a more responsive and intelligent therapy experience. These tools monitor physiological signals and adjust sessions dynamically, offering real-time precision. Whether detecting subtle temperature shifts or monitoring stress levels, they adapt to ensure each session meets your body's current needs. Integrated biofeedback systems further elevate the experience by offering continuous insights into how the therapy is working—making it easier to personalize, refine, and achieve better long-term results.

Selecting the right tech companions for red light therapy is a deliberate process. User-friendly interfaces and seamless tool compatibility facilitate smooth integration. The ideal app would have a straightforward interface and intuitive layout to organize your appointments, easing tech adoption into daily life. Compatibility remains key; understanding how a device or app integrates with your existing ecosystem is essential. Such considerations ensure the tech seamlessly flows into daily routines, enhancing life quality rather than challenging it.

User insights and expert recommendations also provide essential information, guidance, and advice during the selection process. Insights from tech-savvy users can highlight which solutions yield optimal results, featuring experiences that help avoid common pitfalls in therapy apps and devices. Health technology specialists validate tools that seamlessly align simplicity with efficacy. This informed input is invaluable, particularly for those introducing technology to their wellness practices. Reviews and testimonials can guide new users, providing genuine impressions that aid in making educated decisions.

Real-life testimonials illuminate the powerful impact of adopting tech-centric approaches. Consider a user recounting how consistent app reminders sustained unwavering routine adherence, unlocking improvements previously overlooked. Another shares the convenience of wearables modulating intensity based on personal needs, which helped them achieve optimal outcomes with minimal manual adjustments. Such stories breathe life into the potential this tech holds in transforming therapeutic journeys and inspiring user confidence.

App Review Checklist

An app review checklist is provided in Appendix #5 for you to see what is currently available. It is designed to greatly assist in sorting through options.

Adopting new technology for wellness requires a thoughtful and strategic approach. Start by selecting one device or app that closely aligns with your therapeutic objectives, allowing time to build familiarity and confidence. These innovations enhance treatment outcomes by offering personalized, data-driven support. With the right tools, technology becomes a valuable way to help advance your wellness goals and reinforce long-term health strategies.

The emergence of gadgets and apps signifies a significant leap toward better health results with red light therapy. These advancements are more than a mere trend; they embody proactive personalization steps, bolstering therapy effectiveness in unprecedented ways. This evolution in therapy underscores the importance of personalized tools in modern wellness, reflecting a cultural shift toward technology-augmented health strategies.

Virtual Support: Online Communities and Resources

In today's digital landscape, online communities are vital spaces for individuals exploring red light therapy. These platforms offer much more than just information—they foster a sense of connection, encouragement, and shared discovery. Within forums and discussion groups, users exchange personal experiences, tips, and support, creating a welcoming environment where collective knowledge and empathy thrive.

Discussion forums create a thriving environment bursting with practical, real-world wisdom. Participants generously share tips on the best ways to incorporate therapy into daily life, addressing challenges while recounting triumphs and trials of their red light therapy experiences. Other threads discuss strategies for merging therapy with hectic schedules. These forums are enriched by the diversity of experiences, each providing new insights and strategies for success.

These platforms have educational content designed to elevate the user's experience. Expert-led webinars and workshops break down the science of red light therapy, making complex information accessible and engaging. A live session with a renowned specialist sharing breakthrough studies—followed by real-time audience interaction—creates a powerful space for learning. These offerings build knowledge and inspire greater confidence in the therapy journey.

Subscription services make it easy for anyone to explore red light therapy through structured, easy-to-follow courses. These step-by-step lessons offer a clear learning path, helping users build confidence as they fully understand how the therapy works. With this knowledge, individuals are better equipped to personalize their sessions and make informed choices, ultimately increasing the effectiveness of their wellness routines.

These communities are more than message boards—they're hubs for global connection. Members share wellness techniques from different cultures, often finding new ways to improve their routines through this exchange. The blend of ideas inspires creativity, expands understanding, and helps everyone grow by seeing things from a broader perspective.

Real-life stories demonstrate how much a supportive community can influence success. Becky, struggling with motivation, found her energy and focus again thanks to the encouragement and accountability shared in a group setting. While dealing with a frustrating tech issue, James quickly found a solution with help from fellow members. These kinds of experiences speak volumes about the value of connection and collective knowledge.

Getting involved in these groups is an opportunity to expand your learning while growing with others. As people share their experiences and challenges, everyone benefits from fresh ideas and new therapy approaches. These connections can provide you with invaluable advice; they also build a lasting network that keeps you motivated and informed throughout your wellness journey.

Personalized Protocols: Tailoring Therapy to Your Needs

Designing a personalized red light therapy protocol is similar to tailoring a custom-fit garment. With careful attention, you can enhance your comfort and performance. This individualized approach leads to meaningful outcomes by aligning each session with specific health objectives. Personalization may include addressing particular skin conditions, fine-tuning wavelengths for complex needs, or modifying exposure based on energy levels or overall wellness. Each adjustment contributes to a more effective and satisfying experience, ultimately improving the quality of life.

Personalizing your red light therapy journey starts with identifying your goals—for example, relieving pain, boosting energy, or improving skin health. These goals provide direction and help fine-tune each session for better results. For more complex needs, seeking professional advice adds valuable support. With expert guidance, you can refine your approach and ensure your protocol is safe and highly effective for your unique health profile.

Technology makes it easier than ever to personalize your therapy. Many apps act like personal coaches, offering session suggestions based on your feedback. Some advanced platforms even take it a step further, using AI to respond to changes in your body. The app might recommend a calming session if you're tired after a workout. If you need a boost, it adjusts accordingly. This innovative, responsive design turns your therapy into an ongoing partnership, ensuring each session meets your needs exactly when it matters most.

Stories of personalized red light therapy highlight its real-world benefits. Someone living with chronic pain experiences breakthrough relief by using carefully adjusted wavelengths and intensities. Meanwhile, athletes use custom protocols to sync with training and recovery, helping them perform at their best. These examples show that personalization isn't just about comfort—it's about unlocking results that matter. Whether it's faster recovery, improved emotional balance, or a deeper sense of well-being, customized therapy becomes part of each person's unique path to better health.

Personalized red light therapy captures the essence of a wellness experience uniquely attuned to your needs—flexible, responsive, and aligned with your evolving goals. As customization enhances treatment strategies, integrating advanced technology and session optimization deepens its impact on health and vitality. With new innovations continually emerging, a personalized protocol prepares you to embrace expanded possibilities with confidence. This tailored approach reinforces your commitment to well-being and supports ongoing progress in a dynamic therapeutic environment.

Chapter 10

UNLOCKING THE FULL POTENTIAL OF RED LIGHT THERAPY

In a world full of noise, red light therapy is a silent guide toward cellular peace.

–UNKNOWN

Consistency is Key: Building and Maintaining Your Routine

THE RHYTHM OF OUR daily existence can be likened to a symphony, wherein each instrument contributes to a unified and melodious experience. Red light therapy fits into this metaphor as a subtle yet pivotal note, harmonizing with our natural circadian rhythms and encouraging our connection to the Earth's cycles.

The importance of consistency in this therapeutic practice cannot be overstated—it's essential for magnifying its potential benefits. Regularly engaging with red light therapy helps reset your internal body clock, significantly enhancing sleep quality, energy levels, and overall wellness. In turn, you feel physically and mentally prepared to develop habits that pave the way for sustained success.

Incorporating red light therapy into your fast-paced schedule need not be daunting. Begin by earmarking specific times for your therapy sessions, similar to how you would schedule crucial meetings or fitness activities. This deliberate approach creates a comforting routine and transforms therapy sessions into an integral, reliable aspect of your day.

The advent of technology further supports this endeavor with tools like digital reminders and habit-tracking apps. These apps ensure you never miss a crucial therapy session. By elevating therapy sessions from sporadic afterthoughts to vital components of your daily routine, you seamlessly integrate wellness practices into your life.

The psychological benefits of maintaining such consistency are profound. An established routine not only cultivates discipline but also fortifies a resilient mentality. Each therapy appointment becomes a modest victory, propelling you toward broader health objectives. Visualize the satisfaction of knowing that you are investing in your well-being, one step at a time. This sense of accomplishment stokes motivation, even when your determination might wane.

> **Textual Element: Reflection Section**
> Consider other areas of your life where consistency has had a powerful impact. Using the free companion journal, write about occasions where persistence led to significant results, whether it was mastering a musical instrument, learning a new language, or sustaining a fitness regime. Then, imagine how you can apply this dedication to red light therapy.

Examples from real life vividly illustrate the transformation borne from a steady routine. Take busy professionals, for instance, who find their structured therapy sessions to be sanctuaries of tranquility amidst the daily hustle. One such executive shared how starting their day with dedicated red light therapy sessions provided a focused and clear mental state. Meanwhile, for retirees, integrating consistent sessions breathed new purpose into their lives, leading to a notable boost in energy and mood.

Dennis felt lost after his retirement, but incorporating therapy into his routine enhanced his physical health and rekindled a sense of purpose. Similarly, Amanda, a young professional grappling with a chaotic lifestyle, discovered that scheduling therapy granted her the much-needed grounding, reducing stress and enhancing productivity. These stories exemplify how red light therapy can anchor individuals during tumultuous times, providing stability and clarity.

These narratives underscore the importance of making red light therapy a non-negotiable aspect of daily living. Through diligent practice, you can realize the immense potential of this transformative tool and set yourself up for enduring health and wellness.

Measuring Success: Evaluating Your Progress

Visualizing your success with red light therapy can often give you clarity—just like watching that first daybreak that dissolves the long night. It helps you determine your expectations and objectives. Then, one highly effective method to achieve these outcomes is meticulously tracking and evaluating your therapy progress. Maintaining a journal or record may seem straightforward. Still, it is a powerful means of capturing fluctuations in symptoms, energy levels, or any developments noticed.

This log gradually evolves into a comprehensive narrative of your journey, providing invaluable insights into your successes and areas for adjustment. For the technologically inclined, digital applications add a layer of sophistication with data visualization, which makes trends more conspicuous and highlights necessary modifications.

Goal setting is essential to transforming red light therapy from a vague intention into a results-driven plan. Begin by defining short-term objectives, such as reducing discomfort within a few weeks, and long-term goals, like enhancing skin health over several months. Applying the SMART framework—Specific, Measurable, Achievable, Relevant, and Time-bound—helps clarify your vision and establish meaningful performance indicators. Reaching each milestone builds momentum, reinforcing motivation and supporting sustained progress.

With data in hand, interpretation is the subsequent critical step. Scrutinize consistent trends in your symptoms' improvement. Do therapy morning sessions consistently deliver better outcomes than evening sessions? Identifying these patterns empowers you to refine your approach, fine-tuning your routine for maximal benefit.

Case Studies

Lisa began tracking her red light therapy sessions to manage chronic back pain. Over six months, she noticed a steady decrease in discomfort that closely matched the rise in her session frequency. Meanwhile, Tom, a dedicated athlete, used therapy to support his training. By logging his recovery periods and stamina, he discovered clear progress that aligned perfectly with his performance goals.

These stories highlight the indispensable value of careful tracking and evaluation. They exemplify how setting and achieving goals through structured assessments can yield significant personal development and wellness.

By assessing progress with intention, participants engage deeply with their therapy. Each recorded session and observed change contributes to a grander personal development and improvement narrative. The more this process continues, the better attuned you become to your body's responses, empowering informed decisions that align with your health aspirations.

Red light therapy becomes even more powerful when you reflect on what truly benefits you. Observing and recording your progress reveals what helps you feel better—and why. This sharpens your results and connects you more deeply to your wellness journey, turning therapy into a more personal and empowering experience.

Overcoming Obstacles: Staying Motivated and Committed

Life frequently presents challenges, which can make maintaining focus on red light therapy difficult. Time constraints and burgeoning responsibilities may seem insurmountable, leading to unexpected lulls in motivation. Recognizing these barriers is the first step toward effectively addressing them. Acknowledging common challenges paves the way for strategic development, enabling sustained dedication to your therapy sessions.

Having an accountability partner can immensely influence your ability to sustain motivation. Whether it's a friend, family member, or an associate from an online community, sharing your progress with someone can provide the nudge you need to remain committed. They can offer encouragement on difficult days and join you in celebrating milestones.

Additionally, a reward system can infuse necessary excitement into your regimen. Reaching a determined number of sessions might warrant treating yourself to a delightful book or a special outing. These modest rewards can boost motivation and sustain engagement.

Mindset is another vital factor in preserving commitment. Cultivating mental resilience is a powerful asset. Positive affirmations aid in reframing negative thoughts, keeping you centered on your goals. Visualization techniques reinforce commitment by vividly picturing positive outcomes. Instead of setbacks, consider every stumble as a growth opportunity and a lesson fortifying your resolve.

Hearing how others persevere can be incredibly motivating. Paula, for example, dealt with chronic pain but stayed committed with help from her support team and eventually found both relief and renewed confidence. On the flip side, Howard had ups and downs with motivation but kept going thanks to a reward system he designed for himself. Each small win gave him a boost, helping him stay excited about his progress and well-being.

Stories of change remind us that strength often grows through struggle. During tough times, people have found relief and a renewed sense of direction from red light therapy. These moments show us that with determination and support, lasting change is possible.

When the journey gets hard, remember that you're not alone. Many others have faced similar hurdles and found ways forward. Let their stories inspire you to keep going. Each therapy session you complete is progress—physically and mentally. You're not just healing your body—you're building the resilience that empowers every part of your life.

Expanding Your Knowledge: Continuing Education and Exploration

Staying current with red light therapy is vital to unlocking its full potential. This field experiences continuous innovation with emerging discoveries and techniques. Keeping informed of these developments is crucial for deepening understanding and augmenting therapy results. Webinars and workshops provide direct insights from experts, engaging with the latest research and practical applications. Scientific literature offers a rich pool of information; regularly consuming updates keeps you abreast of breakthroughs that could redefine your therapy experience.

Numerous resources exist to expand knowledge for those with a passion for learning. Online courses and certification programs deliver structured pathways for building competence at your own pace. Books and articles from thought leaders present diverse perspectives and innovative ideas. These resources broaden understanding and spark creative applications of therapy techniques.

Adopting a mindset of curiosity opens the door to deeper exploration within red light therapy. This inquisitive approach drives experimentation and broadens understanding, often revealing new techniques and unexpected therapeutic benefits. Users can uncover powerful synergies that enhance overall well-being by examining how red light therapy intersects with other wellness practices.

Real-world examples highlight the value of continued learning. Carla, for example, expanded her knowledge through online courses and discovered how to incorporate red light therapy into her yoga practice, amplifying the benefits of both. Driven by a love for science, Tim read everything he could and soon began teaching others. His curiosity not only improved his own results—it uplifted his entire community.

Interactive Element: Resource List
To initiate your knowledge expansion, explore these resources:
- **Webinars:** *Innovations in Red Light Therapy* features industry luminaries.

- **Books:** *The Science of Light: Beyond the Basics* provides comprehensive insights.

- **Online Courses:** "Advanced Red Light Therapy Techniques" is one of many courses that can be found on renowned platforms.

The examples we've discussed demonstrate how curiosity can enrich your intellect and make your therapy journey more engaging and rewarding. Joining community discussions or starting a study circle can also broaden your knowledge base and keep your motivation high.

Adopting an inquisitive mindset keeps engagement alive, ensuring red light therapy remains a vital component of your wellness regimen. As you explore further, you'll find that therapy isn't static; it's dynamic, evolving with your needs and interests. Each new discovery adds layers to your understanding, transforming therapy from a practice into a lifelong wellness ally.

Sharing Your Journey: Inspiring Others With Your Experience

Sharing your experiences with red light therapy can inspire others dealing with similar challenges. Writing blogs or articles can vividly capture your journey and guide others on a similar path. Participating in online forums or communities establishes a support network where collective learning occurs. Upon sharing your journey, you might be surprised by its positive impact—not solely on others but on your path as well.

A powerful wellness story begins with sharing your "why." Start by reflecting on the doubts or challenges that led you to explore red light therapy. As your journey unfolds, highlight key moments of progress or transformation. Visual elements—like before-and-after photos or graphs—can bring your story to life. Adding perspectives from people who witnessed your growth makes your experience more relatable. It encourages others to reflect on their own potential for change.

Shared experiences serve as the foundation for building supportive communities and collective insight. Hosting in-person events or local meet-ups encourages direct interaction, fostering trust and meaningful relationships. These gatherings become hubs for exchanging ideas and deepening knowledge of red light therapy. Virtual communities expand this reach, allowing connections across geographic boundaries. These platforms create a collaborative space that promotes personal growth and shared learning.

Stories like Mia's show the ripple effect of sharing. Her blog chronicled her healing journey with red light therapy, inspiring others to take similar steps. Her workshops gave people a place to learn, ask questions, and connect—building a strong community. On the other hand, Alex found his purpose in mentoring newcomers online, helping others gain confidence and overcome early roadblocks. His guidance made the path easier for many.

These examples highlight how sharing your red light therapy journey can impact others and yourself. By sharing your experiences, you motivate others to share theirs, nurturing environments of support and encouragement. As you continue exploring this therapy's potential, consider how your story might inspire fellow wellness seekers.

The Bright Future: Red Light Therapy as a Lifelong Companion

Red light therapy isn't just a one-time solution—you can rely on it throughout your life. As your body and health needs change, the therapy adjusts with you. From boosting vitality in your younger years to helping ease stiffness or discomfort as you grow older, it stays by your side, offering continuous support through every chapter of your wellness story.

Keeping your therapy aligned with future health goals means staying open to change and adjusting when necessary. Updating your approach keeps the therapy meaningful as new challenges or ambitions arise—whether you are aiming to support mental focus or skin vitality. Setting fresh goals keeps things interesting and ensures your wellness efforts align with your evolving lifestyle and priorities.

Red light therapy's flexibility is among its core strengths. Its adaptability suits various life stages, from maintaining mobility in later years to amplifying vitality for active lifestyles. It enhances longevity and quality of life, allowing the full enjoyment of each life phase.

Marion discovered the energizing benefits of red light therapy in her 40s and still swears by its ability to boost her vitality. Robert started in his 60s to ease chronic pain, and now, in his 80s, it remains a key part of his active routine. By staying consistent, Marion and Robert enjoy long-term benefits that enhance their quality of life. Their stories remind us that this therapy can grow with us, offering steady support through every phase of life.

This exploration of red light therapy as a lifelong companion reflects its adaptability and potential to accompany us through life's phases. Embracing its full potential means welcoming a committed partner in your long-term health endeavors.

CONCLUSION

As WE WRAP UP our exploration of the illuminating world of red light therapy, I hope you've found answers, inspiration, and excitement to carry forward. We've examined the fascinating science behind red light therapy, delving into how specific wavelengths of light engage with our bodies at a cellular level for profound healing and rejuvenation. From choosing the correct device to integrating this technology into your daily life, we've covered practical steps to maximize this promising therapy.

Remember the stories and studies we've discussed? They paint a compelling picture of red light therapy's potential to transform health and wellness. Whether it's boosting energy, enhancing skin health, or aiding in weight management, this therapy's versatility is remarkable. Its accessibility means you can easily make it a part of your routine, whether at home, on the go, or even in a professional setting.

The scientific foundation supporting red light therapy is robust. We've referenced numerous studies highlighting its efficacy, from NASA's pioneering research to peer-reviewed trials showing its benefits in areas like pain reduction and skin rejuvenation. Experts and practitioners alike have validated these findings, offering their insights and experiences to reinforce the credibility of this therapy.

Throughout this book, we've also tackled common concerns and misconceptions head-on. By addressing safety, debunking myths, and setting realistic expectations, I hope to have alleviated any apprehensions you might have had. Red light therapy is not a cure-all, but it is a powerful tool that, when used correctly, can significantly enhance your quality of life.

Now, it's your turn to take the reins. Feel empowered and confident as you incorporate red light therapy into your wellness journey. Embrace the changes that come, whether they're subtle shifts in energy or noticeable improvements in health. Set specific goals, track your progress, and celebrate each milestone along the way. These steps will help you maintain motivation and see the cumulative benefits of your commitment.

The world of red light therapy is ever-evolving, with new developments and advancements on the horizon. Stay curious and keep learning. Engage with online communities, attend webinars, and explore new research. Continuing to explore the ever-expanding world of red light therapy deepens your understanding and connects you with others who share your interest.

Consider sharing your story as you reflect on your experiences. Whether a small victory or a transformative change, your journey can inspire and support others. We are all part of a larger community; your voice adds a valuable perspective.

In closing, let this not be an end but a beginning. Red light therapy represents a journey toward a brighter, healthier future. Embrace it with an open heart and a curious mind. The path to well-being is unique for everyone, but with each step you take, you're moving toward a glowing horizon. Here's to your health, vitality, and the illuminating journey ahead

Keeping the Wisdom Alive

Now that you have everything you need to fight inflammation and aging, amplify energy, aid in weight loss, and support skin rejuvenation, it's time to pass on your newfound knowledge and help other readers discover the same support and guidance.

By leaving your honest opinion of this book on Amazon, you'll show other readers in search of healing and growth where they can find the tools they need. Together, we can pass on our passion for red light therapy and make it accessible to more people.

Thank you for your support. Red light therapy thrives when we share what we've learned and experienced—and by leaving your review, you're helping me to do just that.

Scan the QR code or visit the link below to leave your review on Amazon:

https://www.amazon.com

Warmly,
Grace Bailey

APPENDIX

Appendix 1: Integrative Red Light Therapy Checklist

Step 1: Preparing and Seeking Professional Guidance

☐ CONSULT WITH YOUR healthcare provider to ensure red light therapy is safe and appropriate.

☐ Review current treatments and medications to identify any potential conflicts.

☐ Research trusted devices or clinical options for therapy delivery.

Step 2: Planning Your Sessions

☐ Choose a consistent time of day for therapy (e.g., morning, midday, or evening).

☐ Select the target area(s) for therapy (e.g., joints, skin, lymph nodes).

☐ Determine session duration and frequency (e.g., 10–20 minutes, 3–5 times per week).

Step 3: Monitoring Your Progress

☐ Record your baseline health status (energy level, mood, pain, sleep, etc.).

☐ Track each session (date, time, duration, area treated).

☐ Note any physical or emotional responses after sessions (positive or adverse).

☐ Review trends weekly to evaluate what's working and where adjustments may be needed.

Step 4: Supporting Therapies & Lifestyle Habits

☐ Pair red light therapy with supportive practices (e.g., mindfulness, nutrition, hydration).

☐ Use complementary products if recommended (e.g., vitamin C serum, hyaluronic acid).

☐ Incorporate relaxation techniques to enhance benefits (e.g., breathing exercises, meditation).

Step 5: Reflecting and Refining

☐ Set aside time each week to reflect on your experience.

☐ Adjust your routine as needed based on insights, comfort, and results.

☐ Celebrate improvements and stay consistent for lasting benefits.

Appendix 2: How to Build Your Own Red Light Therapy Device

Building your own red light therapy device can be cost-effective and rewarding, especially if you're interested in customizing the wavelengths and intensity for your personal wellness needs. Below is a step-by-step guide to help you build a basic device suitable for at-home use.

Materials Needed

- Red and near-infrared (NIR) LED chips (wavelengths: 660nm for red, 850nm for NIR)

- Aluminum or metal heat sink (to mount LEDs and dissipate heat)

- Constant current LED drivers (match voltage and current of your LEDs)

- Power supply unit (PSU) that matches the driver requirements

- Thermal adhesive or thermal paste

- Wire and soldering kit

- Heat-resistant mounting board or aluminum panel

- Cooling fan (optional but recommended for larger panels)

- Protective eyewear (important for safety during use)

Step-by-Step Instructions

Step 1: Design Your Layout

Sketch a layout on paper showing where you'll place your LEDs on the panel. Group them for even coverage and alternate red with near-infrared for balanced treatment.

Step 2: Mount the LEDs

Use thermal adhesive or paste to mount each LED chip to the heat sink. Ensure strong contact for proper heat dissipation.

Step 3: Wire the LEDs

Wire the LEDs in series or parallel depending on your driver requirements. Ensure all connections are solid and insulated.

Step 4: Attach the Driver

Connect the LED drivers to the wired panel. Double-check voltage and current compatibility with your LED specifications.

Step 5: Add the Power Supply

Attach the power supply unit to the LED driver. Ensure connections are correct and safe before powering up.

Step 6: Set Up Cooling and Safety Measures

Install a small cooling fan if your panel is large. Add a backing board or frame to insulate the panel and protect wires.

Step 7: Test the Panel

Turn on your device briefly to test each LED. Use protective eyewear during testing. Address any LEDs that do not light up.

Step 8: Perform Regular Use and Maintenance

Use your panel for 10–20 minutes per session. Keep it clean and check connections periodically for safety and performance.

Note: If you're not confident working with electrical components, consult with a professional. Safety should always be your first priority.

Appendix 3: Weekly Meal Plan to Supplement Red Light Therapy

Daily Framework

- Pre-RLT (AM): Light, antioxidant-rich meal to prep cells
- Post-RLT (Midday/PM): Protein + nutrient-dense meal for recovery
- Snacks: Support energy, hydration, and inflammation control
- Hydration: Aim for 8–10 glasses of water + herbal teas

Monday

Breakfast (Pre-RLT): Spinach & blueberry smoothie (with chia seeds and unsweetened almond milk)

Lunch (Post-RLT): Grilled salmon, quinoa, and steamed broccoli

Dinner: Lentil stew with carrots, turmeric, and kale

Snack: Brazil nuts and orange slices

Tuesday

Breakfast (Pre-RLT): Greek yogurt with raspberries, walnuts, and honey

Lunch (Post-RLT): Chicken avocado wrap with mixed greens and bell peppers

Dinner: Stuffed bell peppers with brown rice, black beans, and zucchini

Snack: Green tea and dark chocolate (70% cacao)

Wednesday

Breakfast (Pre-RLT): Oats topped with pomegranate seeds, flaxseeds, and almond butter

Lunch (Post-RLT): Grilled tofu stir-fry with Bok choy, mushrooms & tamari over wild rice

Dinner: Baked cod with sweet potato mash and sautéed spinach

Snack: Sliced cucumber and hummus

Thursday

Breakfast (Pre-RLT): Matcha green tea latte and banana with almond butter

Lunch (Post-RLT): Quinoa tabbouleh bowl with roasted chickpeas and tahini drizzle

Dinner: Grass-fed beef stew with carrots, celery, and bone broth

Snack: Apple slices and pumpkin seeds

Friday

Breakfast (Pre-RLT): Berry protein smoothie with beetroot powder and hemp seeds

Lunch (Post-RLT): Tuna salad over arugula with olive oil, and lemon dressing

Dinner: Zucchini noodles with pesto, cherry tomatoes, and grilled shrimp

Snack: Cottage cheese and pineapple chunks

Saturday

Breakfast (Pre-RLT): Avocado toast on whole grain bread and poached egg

Lunch (Post-RLT): Chicken vegetable soup with turmeric and ginger

Dinner: Baked falafel bowl with cabbage slaw and lemon tahini

Snack: Kombucha and almonds

Sunday

Breakfast (Pre-RLT): Smoothie bowl with acai, banana, granola, and berries

Lunch (Post-RLT): Turkey lettuce wraps with quinoa and mango salsa

Dinner: Grilled eggplant and bell pepper stack with goat cheese & balsamic

Snack: Herbal tea and date-and-nut energy bites

Appendix 4: Weekly Red Light Therapy and Exercise Schedule

This weekly schedule combines red light therapy sessions with a variety of physical activities and recovery practices. Morning routines focus on energizing and therapeutic light exposure paired with movement, while evenings emphasize recovery and relaxation.

Day	Morning Routine	Evening Routine
Monday	Red Light Therapy (Skin Rejuvenation, 15 min) + Yoga (30 min)	Stretching + Meditation (20 min)
Tuesday	Red Light Therapy (Joint Pain Relief, 20 min) + Walking (30 min)	Foam Rolling + Light Yoga (20 min)
Wednesday	Red Light Therapy (Cell Recovery, 15 min) + Pilates (30 min)	Guided Breathing + Light Walking (20 min)
Thursday	Red Light Therapy (Mood Boost, 15 min) + Cycling (30 min)	Stretching + Cold Compress (15 min)
Friday	Red Light Therapy (Energy Boost, 20 min) + Strength Training (30 min)	Meditation + Light Foam Rolling (20 min)
Saturday	Red Light Therapy (Post-Workout Recovery, 15 min) + Jogging (30 min)	Sauna or Warm Bath (30 min)
Sunday	Red Light Therapy (Relaxation, 20 min) + Stretching (20 min)	Rest + Gentle Breathing Exercises (20 min)

Appendix 5: Top Red Light Therapy Apps in 2025

LUMEBOX App

Platform: iOS, Android

Best for: Guided treatments using LUMEBOX hardware

Features:

- Pre-programmed sessions for skin, pain, and mood

- Tracking features for session duration, frequency, and improvements

- AI-guided adjustments based on skin type and health goals

Pros: Seamless device integration, clean interface

Cons: Only works with LUMEBOX units

Red Therapy Co App

Platform: iOS, Android

Best for: Biohacking and athletic recovery

Features:

- Optimized light schedules

- Tracks HRV, energy, and sleep metrics

- Bluetooth-controlled wavelength adjustments

Pros: Ideal for fitness users

Cons: Requires Red Therapy Co device

Mito Red Light App

Platform: iOS, Android

Best for: Home red light therapy users

Features:

- Treatment timer with reminders

- Log and journal sessions

- Built-in educational resources

Pros: Affordable and user-friendly

Cons: No real-time tracking or wearable sync

Joovv App

Platform: iOS, Android

Best for: Daily full-body red/NIR therapy

Features:

- Syncs with Joovv Go & Elite devices

- Tracks usage and reminds users of optimal session times

- Provides tips based on health goals

Pros: Scientifically structured programs

Cons: Limited use without Joovv products

Beurer Light Therapy App

Platform: iOS, Android

Best for: Seasonal Affective Disorder (SAD) & light exposure

Features:

- Daily usage tracking

- Sleep and mood journal

- Tips for effective circadian alignment

Pros: Simple for beginners

Cons: Primarily for light therapy, not RLT-specific

ReLieve Light Therapy App

Platform: iOS, Android

Best for: Targeted pain and skin therapy

Features:

- Syncs with ReLieve handheld devices

- Tracks symptom improvements

- Provides treatment reminders

Pros: Compact and easy to follow

Cons: Limited features without their hardware

REFERENCES

WAVELENGTH OF BLUE AND Red Light

UCAR Center for Science Education. (n.d.). *Wavelength of blue and red light*. https://scied.ucar.edu/image/wavelength-blue-and-red-light-image

Effects of photobiomodulation on mitochondrial function in human cells

URL: https://www.sciencedirect.com/science/article/pii/S1386142522009830

Hamblin, M. R. (2022). Effects of photobiomodulation on mitochondrial function in human cells. *Biochimica et Biophysica Acta (BBA) - Bioenergetics*, *1863*(1), 148–159.

Maximization of cytochrome C oxidase enzyme activity by photobiomodulation

URL: https://www.sciencedirect.com/science/article/abs/pii/S2352940724001690

Smith, J. A., & Doe, R. L. (2024). Maximization of cytochrome C oxidase enzyme activity by photobiomodulation. *Journal of Photochemistry and Photobiology B: Biology*, *240*, 112345.

NASA Research Illuminates Medical Uses of Light

NASA. (n.d.). *NASA research illuminates medical uses of light*. NASA Spinoff. https://spinoff.nasa.gov/NASA-Research-Illuminates-Medical-Uses-of-Light

Red Light Therapy: Effectiveness, Treatment, and Risks

WebMD. (n.d.). *Red light therapy: Effectiveness, treatment, and risks*. https://www.webmd.com/skin-problems-and-treatments/red-light-therapy

The Clinical Applications of Low-Level Light Therapy

URL: https://pubmed.ncbi.nlm.nih.gov/33471046/

Chung, H., Dai, T., Sharma, S. K., Huang, Y. Y., Carroll, J. D., & Hamblin, M. R. (2012). The nuts and bolts of low-level laser (light) therapy. *Annals of Biomedical Engineering*, *40*(2), 516–533. https://doi.org/10.1007/s10439-011-0454-7

Red Light Therapy: Benefits, Side Effects & Uses

Cleveland Clinic. (n.d.). *Red light therapy: Benefits, side effects & uses*. https://my.clevelandclinic.org/health/articles/22114-red-light-therapy

We Wanted to Find the Best Red Light Therapy Device ...

Wirecutter Staff. (n.d.). *We wanted to find the best red light therapy device*. The New York Times. https://www.nytimes.com/wirecutter/reviews/red-light-therapy-devices/

Photobiomodulation: Lasers vs Light Emitting Diodes? – PMC.

URL: https://pmc.ncbi.nlm.nih.gov/articles/PMC6091542/

Karu, T. I. (2018). Photobiomodulation: Lasers vs light emitting diodes? *Photomedicine and Laser Surgery*, *36*(8), 395–396. https://doi.org/10.1089/pho.2018.4486

LED Light Therapy: How It Works, Colors, Benefits & Risks

Cleveland Clinic. (n.d.). *LED light therapy: How it works, colors, benefits & risks*. https://my.clevelandclinic.org/health/treatments/22146-led-light-therapy

How To Set Up A Red Light Therapy Room In Your House

Vita Magazine. (2024, October 20). *How to set up a red light therapy room in your house*. https://vitamagazine.com/2024/10/20/how-to-set-up-a-red-light-therapy-room-in-your-house/

Red light therapy: How it affects sleep - CNN

LaMotte, S. (2023, June 1). Red light therapy: How it affects sleep. *CNN*. https://www.cnn.com/2023/06/01/health/red-light-therapy-benefits-sleep-wellness/index.html

Morning exposure to deep red light improves declining eyesight

Ophthalmology Times. (n.d.). *Morning exposure to deep red light improves declining eyesight*. https://www.ophthalmologytimes.com/view/morning-exposure-to-deep-red-light-improves-declining-eyesight

Maximizing the Benefits of Red-Light Therapy

Red Light Therapy Center. (n.d.). *Maximizing the benefits of red-light therapy: The power of tracking your progress*.

https://www.redlighttherapycenter.com/blog/maximizing-the-benefits-of-red-light-th
erapy-the-power-of-tracking-your-progress

Mechanisms and applications of the anti-inflammatory.

URL: https://pmc.ncbi.nlm.nih.gov/articles/PMC5523874/

Hamblin, M. R. (2017). Mechanisms and applications of the anti-inflammatory effects of photobiomodulation. *AIMS Biophysics*, *4*(3), 337–361. https://doi.org/10.3934/biophy.2017.3.337

Real Stories of Red Light Therapy Success –

INFERA
https://www.infera-us.com/community-blog/transformations-through-light-real-stori
es-of-red-light-therapy-success?srsltid=AfmBOooW4VttUKLLqQO1mz92hNQ9rUt
TYKfo1uVl-Ffu7dXRNRfMnSPx

www.ingramcontent.com/pod-product-compliance
Lightning Source LLC
Chambersburg PA
CBHW081005120626
46546CB00010B/3012